COMPLETE
LEARNING DISABILITIES
HANDBOOK

COMPLETE LEARNING DISABILITIES HANDBOOK

Ready-to-Use Techniques for Teaching Learning-Handicapped Students

Joan M. Harwell

THE CENTER FOR APPLIED
RESEARCH IN EDUCATION
West Nyack, New York 10995

10 9 8 7 6

ISBN 0-87628-239-7

THE CENTER FOR APPLIED
RESEARCH IN EDUCATION
BUSINESS & PROFESSIONAL DIVISION
A division of Simon & Schuster
West Nyack, New York 10995

Printed in the United States of America

The Practical Help This Book Offers

My purpose in writing the *Complete Learning Disabilities Handbook* is to share with you some of the things I have learned in my twenty-four years of working with learning-disabled students.

ABOUT LEARNING DISABILITIES

Learning disability is the term currently being used by educators and physicians to describe a group of conditions that interfere with a person's learning and functioning in life, as shown in the following two situations:

1. Tears welled up in the eyes of the young mother as she told me of her concern regarding her son's educational progress: "I don't want him to have the awful experiences I had." She went on to describe the feelings of the typical learning-disabled person. "I grew up thinking I was dumb. It is only now that I feel I have any value as a person."

2. Several years ago, a young man told me of the subterfuge he had contrived to get and hold a job as a mechanic. He bought some glasses even though he didn't need them and wore them for a while. Thereafter, when he had to read, he'd use various excuses, such as "I broke my glasses," "I forgot my glasses," and so on. People would read to him. It was some time before his employer realized that this young man was not able to read.

Dr. Samuel Kirk was the first to use the term *learning disabilities* (often abbreviated LD) in 1963. Prior to that time, labels such as *minimal brain damage* (MBD) and *minimal brain dysfunction* had been used. In the early 1940s, physicians speculated that brain damage accounted for the difficulty some children experienced. When research did not support that theory, doctors decided that perhaps some parts of the brain did not function as they should. Later information led to the adoption of terms to describe a specific kind of learning difficulty, such as *dyslexia* (reading difficulty), *dyscalculia* (mathematics difficulty), and *dysgraphia* (writing problems).

Whatever it is called, people with a learning disability find their performance in life hampered. They must work harder than the nonhandicapped. When they are finished, they may find their product negatively criticized by their teacher, parent, or employer. Worse yet, they may be perfectionists and lose respect for their own work. Rejection (whether internal or external) results in self-devaluation, frustration, anger, depression, or anxiety.

Learning disabilities is a relatively new field. Those of us in it are pioneers. We should recognize that there are no experts, but rather many people with ideas to share. As we move forward, we have to test new theories and beliefs, discarding or refining them as we gain additional information.

ABOUT THE HANDBOOK

The aim of this handbook is to give you useful information regarding the diagnosis and remediation of learning disabilities. Designed for all in-service elementary and secondary educators, it seeks to provide practical suggestions to make work with learning-disabled students and their parents more effective. Experienced regular teachers and specialists will find many ideas for use in their daily lesson planning. And beginning teachers, too, should find the handbook invaluable.

For easy use, the handbook is organized into the following seven chapters:

Chapter 1, "Learning Disabilities—An Overview," presents a brief historical review and gives answers to questions such as "What is it?", "What causes it?", "How many people have it?", and "What is the prognosis?"

Chapter 2, "Identification and Planning to Meet Student Needs," reviews the identification process, gives insight into typical parental feelings about the condition, provides assistance in developing a workable Individual Education Plan (IEP), and explores the roles of a multitude of professionals in the planning phase.

Chapter 3, "Classroom Management," guides the teacher in the areas of classroom and behavioral management: how to design lessons that teach quickly how to choose effective instructional materials, and how to group students for instruction.

Chapter 4, "Intervention with Learning-Disabled Students," focuses on ways to help students with particular learning disabilities, including negative self-esteem, visual and auditory perceptual deficits, deficits in spatial awareness, conceptual deficits, poor memory, and attention deficit disorder.

Chapter 5, "Intervention in Specific Subject Areas," gives pointers on how to teach reading, spelling, writing skills, and math and reference skills. These sections were written to answer teachers' questions in these areas. Included are sample goals to help in the development of the Individual Education Plan and sample lesson activities.

Chapter 6, "Working with Older Learning-Disabled Students," explores intervention with the older student beginning with grade 4 and moving on through intermediate school and high school and into the collegiate or vocational training phase of the student's life. Included in this chapter are suggestions for helping LD students to understand their disability (recognize their strengths), to develop their own strategies for learning, and to become their own advocate.

Chapter 7, "A Call to Action," reminds us again that learning disabilities is a relatively new field and that we still have much to learn. It is also a plea to explore some changes in the law that would benefit the learning-disabled person.

The handbook ends with a glossary, a list of testing materials, a list of sources of help, an educator's checklist of clues to vision problems, and an index designed to speed access to a particular topic.

I hope that you find the *Complete Learning Disabilities Handbook* a valuable, quick reference tool for all aspects of your work with learning-disabled students.

Joan M. Harwell

About the Author

Joan M. Harwell has over twenty-four years of experience as a regular classroom teacher and special education teacher for educationally handicapped children in the public schools of San Bernardino, California. She has also run several successful remedial programs for slow and reluctant learners and has authored one prior book in the field, *How to Diagnose and Correct Learning Difficulties in the Classroom* (Parker Publishing Company, 1982).

Harwell earned her B.A. from San Jose State College and an M.A. from the University of Redlands. Currently, she is a learning-handicapped Resource Specialist in an elementary school and also a mentor teacher.

Contents

THE PRACTICAL HELP THIS BOOK OFFERS v

CHAPTER 1 LEARNING DISABILITIES – AN OVERVIEW 1

Definition 3
Historical Perspective 3
Incidence 3
Causes 5

Symptomology Checklist

Visual Perceptual Deficits
Visual Perceptual/Visual Motor Deficits
Auditory Perceptual Deficits
Spatial Relationship/Body Awareness Deficits
Conceptual Deficits
Memory Deficits
Motor Output Deficits
Behavioral Components

Prognosis 10

**CHAPTER 2 INDENTIFICATION AND PLANNING
TO MEET STUDENT NEEDS** 11

Initiating a Request for Help 13
Understanding Parental Feelings 16

Student Study Team Process—Flowchart 17

Student Study Team 18

Student Study Team Process—Format for a Typical Meeting 21

The Multidisciplinary Process – Format Assessment 25

Referral Process—Flowchart 27

Guidlines for Assessment 28

Intellectual Assessment
Academic Assessment
Learning Style Assessment

Health Assessment
Social Assessment

Individual Education Plan   43

Determining Appropriate Educational Setting
Writing an Individual Education Plan

Dissenting Opinions   45
Due Process   46
Parents' Rights   46
Role of Case Carrier in Monitoring Student Progress   47

Sample of an Individual Education Plan

CHAPTER 3 CLASSROOM MANAGEMENT   51

Environmental Decisions   53

How to Create a Utilitarian and Attractive Classroom

Behavioral Management Considerations   54

First Week Activities
Establishing Rules
Creating Positive Feeling Tone
Finding Better Ways to Talk to Children
Providing Alternatives for Faster Students
Providing Alternatives for Slower Students
Preventing Misbehavior
*Value of Positive and Negative Reinforcers and the Use
of Extinction*
Four Types of Difficult Students
Handling Misbehavior

Academic Management Considerations   66

Academic Enhancers
Involving the Parents in Meaningful Ways
Involving the Principal in a Positive Way
The Case for Cooperative Learning
Providing Adequate Learning Opportunities
Increasing Retention
*Use of Higher Level Questions, Imagery, Visualization,
and Verbalization*
Probing and Thinking Time
Effective Lesson Design

Importance of Setting Goals
What Steps Should a Good Lesson Include?
Visualization and Verbalization Cards
Teacher Self-Evaluation

CHAPTER 4 INTERVENTION WITH LEARNING-DISABLED STUDENTS   85

**Techniques for Eliminating Failure Syndrome
and Building Positive Self-Esteem   87**
**Techniques for Visual Perceptual Deficits
and Visual Motor Deficits   92**
Techniques for Remediating Auditory Perceptual Deficits   99
Techniques for Eliminating Perseveration   100
**Techniques for Remediating Deficits in Spatial Awareness
and Body Awareness   100**
Techniques for Removing Conceptual Deficits   103
Techniques for Improving Memory   106
**Techniques for Assisting the Student
with Attention Deficit Disorder   108**

CHAPTER 5 INTERVENTION IN SPECIFIC SUBJECT AREAS   113

Teaching the LD Student Penmanship   115
Teaching the LD Student to Read   117

Teaching the Young Student
Teaching the Older Student
Teaching New Vocabulary
General Principles for Reading

Teaching Spelling Skills to LD Students   141
Teaching Writing Skills to LD Students   146

Suggested Topics for Student Writing

Pointers for Helping the LD Child in Math   155
Teaching Reference Skills   171

Dictionary
Thesaurus
Indexes
Card Catalog
Maps and Atlases
Encyclopedias

**CHAPTER 6 WORKING WITH OLDER LEARNING
DISABLED STUDENTS   179**

      Teaching Strategies for Success   181
      **Understanding the Changing Needs of the Intermediate LD
      Student   187**
      **Adjusting and Developing Curriculum to Meet Student
      Interest   188**
      **Developing Vocational Awareness, Prevocational Skills,
      and Vocational Skills   188**
      The Art of Counseling Intermediate Students   189
      The Art of Counseling Secondary Students   190
      Helping Parents Cope   190
      Understanding the Needs of the Secondary Student   191
      College and Vocational Training   191

CHAPTER 7 A CALL TO ACTION   193

GLOSSARY   201

TEST MATERIALS   203

SOURCES OF HELP   205

EDUCATOR'S CHECKLIST OF CLUES TO VISION PROBLEMS   207

1

LEARNING DISABILITIES— AN OVERVIEW

DEFINITION

Learning disability (LD) and *learning handicap* (LH) are terms I use interchangeably to describe individuals who:

1. can see;
2. can hear;
3. have general intelligence in the near-average, average, or above-average range;
4. have educational difficulties that do not stem from inadequate educational experience or cultural factors; and
5. do not acquire and use information efficiently due to some impairment in perception, conceptualization, language, memory, attention, or motor control.

In my opinion, the term *learning disabled* is an unfortunate label because it implies a condition that cannot be overcome. That implication produces a sense of hopelessness. Moreover, we can demonstrate that many learning-disabled persons have learned to compensate for their deficit areas and have made significant contributions to society; therefore, I prefer the term *learning handicap*—for in learning (as in golf), a handicap is something we may wish to (1) give recognition to, (2) make adjustments for, and (3) allow a person to win in spite of.

People with learning disabilities do not look handicapped—they wear no prosthesis to assist them. The fact that they have no visible handicap has led to this condition being referred to as *the invisible handicap*. Because their difficulties are not obvious, learning-disabled persons are often misunderstood and maligned. They are accused of "not listening," of "being lazy," of "being clumsy," or of "being weird." Not understanding their own problem, they often experience loss of self-esteem and feelings of worthlessness.

HISTORICAL PERSPECTIVE

Historically, the learning-disabled person managed to cope—or didn't manage. I suspect that many of them found jobs in unskilled labor. As the United States passed from an agrarian society to an industrial society and as compulsory school attendance laws were enforced, schools faced the problem of educating slower-learning children. Self-contained

3

classes were established. Educators believed that this isolation was in the best interest of both the handicapped and the nonhandicapped child. Handicapped children got specially trained teachers, special equipment, and a smaller teacher to pupil ratio. The nonhandicapped child's progress would not be hindered by children who learned more slowly.

Research findings in the 1960s were disturbing: Many children who were classified as retarded were found to be socioculturally deprived—but not retarded—when tested with appropriate materials in their native language or in a nonverbal format. Researchers also found that teachers of slow learners were not the best trained teachers and that they rated themselves inferior to their regular class counterparts. It was also found that labeling children hindered their progress. It lowered their self-esteem, and it led their teachers to expect less from them.

In the late 1960s, education shifted from a position where all children in a given class were exposed to the same curriculum, presented to all children in the same way—to a position where instruction was individualized to meet the child's academic placement. Today in a typical third grade class, it is not unusual to find children reading from grade level 1 to grade level 6. Other signs of this shift are learning centers, programmed materials, resource rooms and personnel, and hardware (teaching machines, typewriters, calculators, videotapes, audiovisual equipment, and cassettes). The investigation into learning modalities (also called *learning styles*) reflected a further effort to make education more meaningful to the individual child.

There was a growing awareness of the following:

1. Special class placement carried with it a stigma.

2. The behavior of some special class students was a problem to school authorities because the students tended to imitate each other rather than to imitate their nonhandicapped peers.

3. Special class placement seemed to build barriers between the handicapped and the nonhandicapped and made integration of handicapped adults into the work-world almost impossible.

4. Handicapped children were not generally receiving equal educational opportunities.

Lobbyists for the handicapped in the early 1970s demanded that Congress enact legislation that would correct these wrongs. In 1975, Public Law 94–142 (The Education of All Handicapped Children Act) was passed guaranteeing each handicapped child, ages 3 to 21, a "free," "appropriate" education in the "least restrictive environment."

The intent of Public Law 94–142 was that each handicapped child would receive a quality education—ideally in a regular classroom with their peers. (Some refer to this law as the *mainstreaming law*.) While the intent of the law is noble, some shortcomings can be cited. For example, many teachers have had little or no training working with learning-disabled children. Also most complain that they cannot give the individual attention needed because they have too many students in their classes.

In the early 1980s, the pitiful status of U.S. education was the subject of a report entitled *A Nation at Risk*, which concluded that unless we quickly made significant changes in our educational system, our nation would lose its position as a world leader.

We *can* afford to educate our children—all of our children—because we cannot afford *not* to.

INCIDENCE

How many people have learning disabilities? We really don't know at this point. Estimates range all the way from 2 percent to over 20 percent of the population. It depends on whom you decide to count. Just as there is a continuum in age or income, there is a continuum in learning disabilities, ranging from persons only mildly affected to persons severely affected. As you begin to read about some of these characteristics, you may find yourself saying, "I used to do that" or "Occasionally, I do that now." It is my firm belief that many people are able to compensate for their difficulties. I believe that early intervention is the key to preventing difficulties from becoming disabilities.

CAUSES

In the literature and the research currently available, a number of causes of learning disabilities are being investigated. We now know the following:

1. There seems to be a strong familial factor. It is not uncommon for parents to report that they or a close relative had learning problems, or for us to find that more than one child in a family has the problem.

2. The incidence of learning disabilities increases in children of mothers who experienced difficult pregnancies, or difficult labors. There is also a higher incidence in children born to mothers younger than 16 or older than 40. Also at risk are children of mothers who had used large amounts of drugs and alcohol during pregnancy.

3. Children who experience postbirth traumas may show learning disabilities. Included in this category are children who are deprived of oxygen at birth and those who show neonatal seizures or early sucking problems. Likewise, children who suffer from chronic ear infections, head trauma, or intracranial infection (encephalitis or meningitis) and those who ingest or inhale neurotoxins may become learning disabled. (Another possible cause is oxygen deprivation, such as in cases of near drowning, carbon monoxide poisoning, and cerebrovascular accident.) Severe malnutrition and conditions producing a sustained fever may also be causative factors.

4. The period from birth to age 3 is crucial for language skills development. If during this period children have recurring ear infections coupled with diminished hearing, they may develop a learning disability in the communications area.

Currently there is much interest in exploring the relationship between learning disabilities and deficits in the immune system (hay fever and allergy). Researchers are also looking into the effects of air pollution on the body and the brain.

Research is continuing in the area of diet. A few years ago, Dr. Benjamin Feingold hypothesized that the widespread use of preservatives and artificial food colorings was a major factor causing children to experience difficulty in attending to or concentrating on a task. Today this research lies in disrepute, but we may yet find a diet connection.

Some have suggested that parents and children in modern society converse less (because of TV and because both parents are forced into the workplace), and they believe that this may be having an adverse effect on children. I personally wonder about the wisdom of allowing our children to watch an average of over twenty-six hours of television programming a week (largely cartoons, sitcoms, and shows with violence). First, I believe that excessive TV watching replaces important activities, such as active play (which involves body development and imagination). Second, TV does not require the active listening that radio once required. To follow a plot on radio, you had to listen carefully and convert the words into mental images. This is not true of TV. You can half-listen, half-look, and still follow the story. I believe that children come to school half-listening, half-attending to their teacher. Their comprehension is diminished or faulty; their ability to process oral instruction is impaired.

Finally, in answer to the question, "What causes learning disabilities?" we frequently cannot find anything in a person's background to account for it. As the research improves, we will probably sharpen our understanding of its causes.

As important as it is to try to find and eliminate the causes of LD, it is equally important to do all that we can for the person who already has the condition. Concentrating only on locating the cause in a particular case will probably not help the person experiencing this handicap.

Symptomology Checklist

SYMPTOMOLOGY CHECKLIST—LEARNING DISABILITIES

(Check behaviors seen. Mark: S = sometimes; O = often)

Visual Perceptual Deficits

——— reversals: *b* for *d*, *p* for *q*
——— inversions: *u* for *n*, *w* for *m*
——— yawns while reading
——— complains eyes hurt, itch/rubs eyes
——— complains print blurs while reading
——— turns head or paper at odd angles
——— closes one eye while working
——— cannot copy accurately
——— loses place frequently
——— rereads lines/skips lines
——— does not recognize an object/word if only part of it is shown

___ reading improves with larger print/fewer items on page/uses a marker to exclude portion of page

___ sequencing errors: *was/saw, on/no*

___ does not see main theme in a picture, picks up some minute detail

___ slow to pick up on likenesses-differences in words; changes in environment

___ erases excessively

___ distortions in depth perception

Visual Perceptual/Visual Motor Deficits

___ letters collide with each other/no space between words

___ letters not on line

___ forms letters in strange way

___ mirror writing (hold paper up to mirror and you see it as it should look)

___ cannot color within lines

___ illegible handwriting

___ holds pencil too tightly; often breaks pencil point/crayons

___ cannot cut

___ cannot paste

___ messy papers

Auditory Perceptual Deficits

___ auditory processing: cannot understand conversation or learning delivered at the normal rate/may comprehend if information is repeated very slowly

___ auditory discrimination: does not hear differences in sounds: short *i, e*; plosive sounds *b, p, d, t, c, g, j, n, m*; does not hear final consonants accurately

___ cannot tell direction sound is coming from

___ does not recognize common sounds for what they are

___ cannot filter out extraneous noise; cannot distinguish teacher's voice from others— hears wrong answers, steadfastly maintains "teacher said it" (Some children get very tense in noisy classroom)

___ does not follow directions

___ does not benefit from oral instruction

Spatial Relationships and Body Awareness Deficits

___ gets lost even in familiar surroundings such as school, neighborhood

___ directionality problems, does not always read or write left to right

___ no space between words

___ cannot keep columns straight in math

_____ bumps into things; clumsy, accident prone

_____ does not understand concepts such as *over, under, around, through, first, last, front, back, up, down*

Conceptual Deficits

_____ cannot read social situations, does not understand body language

_____ cannot see relationship between similar concepts

_____ cannot compare how things are alike/different; classification activities are difficult

_____ does not understand time relationships—*yesterday, today, tomorrow, after/before, 15 minutes* versus *2 hours,* "*hurry*"

_____ does not associate an act with its logical consequence. "If I talk, I get detention" (being punished for no reason. Unfair.)

_____ little imagination

_____ no sense of humor; cannot recognize a joke/pun

_____ tends to be expressionless

_____ slow responses

_____ not able to create, to "think," to create poetry, original stories

_____ cannot make closure; cannot read less than clear ditto; cannot finish a sentence such as "I like it when. . . . "; difficulty filling in blanks

_____ excessively gullible

_____ cannot do inferential thinking: What might happen next? Why did this happen?

_____ great difficulty in writing

_____ bizarre answers/or correct answers found in bizarre ways

_____ cannot think in an orderly, logical way

_____ does not understand emotions, concepts such as *beauty, bravery*

_____ classroom comments are often "off track" or reasons in bizarre ways

_____ difficulty grasping number concepts: *more/less;* $>/<$; can't estimate

_____ mispronounces common words

Memory Deficits

_____ cannot remember what was just seen (was shown)

_____ cannot remember what was just heard

_____ cannot remember sequence of 4 numbers given auditorally

_____ cannot copy math problems accurately

_____ cannot remember spelling for common/frequently encountered words

_____ remembers things from long ago but not recent events

_____ poor sight vocabulary—few words known to automatic level

_____ slow to memorize rhymes/poem (makes many errors)

_____ appears to know something one day but doesn't know it the next

___ limited expressive language; does not remember names for objects—"that thing"
___ limited receptive language
___ makes same error again and again; does not seem to benefit from experience
___ writing poor—cannot remember to capitalize, punctuate, skip a line, indent, and so on

Motor Output Deficits

___ perseveration—gives same response again and again (hangs up)
___ distortions in gross motor functions—cannot skip, hop, hit ball, and so on
___ difficulty cutting, pasting, coloring, writing (can point to correct way to form a letter but cannot produce it on paper)
___ can point to correct spelling but cannot copy it accurately
___ can dictate story or paragraph but cannot write it
___ does not communicate orally to a degree appropriate for age
___ mouth noises
___ tics

Behavioral Components

Attention Deficit Disorder

___ good days—bad days
___ cannot sit still
___ cannot stand still
___ impulsive; does not consider consequence before acting
___ low frustration tolerance: short fuse
___ cannot finish assignments in allotted time
___ visually distractible; looks up to all visual stimuli
___ auditorally distractible; responds by looking up to all noise
___ fidgety: drumming fingers, tapping toes, rolling pencil, fooling with objects; makes mouth noises; incessant talking
___ short attention span
___ spaces off—confused—does not sit up/head on desk/"tired"
___ negativistic/oppositional behavior
___ little work produced; daydreams
___ reads something correctly, but mind is elsewhere as evidenced in poor comprehension
___ overreacts to stimuli (cannot mind own business)
___ does not follow rules; often claims didn't hear them
___ may be cruel, mean to others; makes fun of them
___ mood swings
___ disorganized; loses books, papers, lunch box, coat

Failure Syndrome

___ describes self as "dumb"
___ does not take reprimands well
___ tends to avoid group activity
___ avoids activity; does little; claims illness
___ daydreams/withdrawal
___ class clown—acting out behavior
___ immature behavior; babyish, seems younger, dependent

Serious Emotional Overlay

___ explosive, unpredictable, dangerous behavior, lashing out
___ preoccupation with death, destruction; prefers dark colors and red, purple, yellow
___ no work produced coupled with lack of enthusiasm for anything
___ tells bizarre stories and purports they really happened
___ shallow feeling for others
___ cannot distinguish reality from fantasy
___ withdraws; alone; little communication
___ feels "picked on"; uses projection, denial; never assumes responsibility for actions
___ fearful, anxious, insecure, tense

PROGNOSIS

Much can be done to help persons with learning disabilities. We know that the earlier the problem is detected and appropriate intervention given, the better the outcome will be.

We also know that learning disabilities can be compensated for or overcome. Some of our most worthwhile people were learning disabled—Winston Churchill, Thomas Edison, Woodrow Wilson, Hans Christian Anderson, and George Bernard Shaw, to name only a few.

2

IDENTIFICATION AND PLANNING TO MEET STUDENT NEEDS

Sometimes a learning-disabled child is identified at birth. The physician attending the mother or the pediatrician seeing the baby realizes that the baby is at risk and refers the parents to the Easter Seal Society for Crippled Children, a developmental center, or the infant care program/preschool program of the local school district.

Children who are identified early tend to have moderate to severe learning disabilities. In general, however, children with learning difficulties are not identified until they begin some sort of schooling. There, observant teachers note that they are out of step with other children their age.

Children with mild learning disabilities are sometimes never identified. They progress through school, labeled as *underachievers*. Teachers see their obvious ability in their strength areas, but they attribute their poor performance in other areas to a lack of motivation or to laziness. Unfortunately, these youngsters often learn to hate school, to experience a loss of self-esteem, to drop out of school, and to never reach their potential in life. Harangued for being lazy and not understanding why they can't do certain tasks, these children depreciate themselves and go through life convinced that they are dumb. Such a waste of potential!

INITIATING A REQUEST FOR HELP

When a child is having a difficulty—academic, behavioral, social, or with attendance—the teacher can bring this to the attention of the Student Study Team (SST) by completing a request form, as follows.

REQUEST FOR STUDENT STUDY TEAM

Student's name _____ Grade _____

Date of birth _____ Age _____

Referring teacher _____

Reason for referral:

Group test scores for past 2 years:
(Name of test and date and results)

Information regarding current performance:

Relevant personal information:

(Be sure to attach interventions log)

REQUEST FOR STUDENT STUDY TEAM

Student's name _____ Young, boy _____ Grade _ 1 (repeating) _

Date of birth _____ 5/2/79 _____ Age ___ 7 ___

Referring teacher ____ Mr. Keen _____

Reason for referral: Boy is not making progress (reading/spelling) in spite of retention. He seems to know something one day but has forgotten it the next. He reverses *b/d*, *p/q*, *n/u*, and *m/w*. He confuses *on/no*. There are several alphabet letters he cannot recognize. He is highly distractible, gets no work done unless I sit with him. He cannot cut and paste.

Group test scores for past 2 years:
(Name of test and date and results)

CTBS (California Test of Basic Skills) 1986 (gr. 1) reading total   1 %tile
math total   1 %tile

Information regarding current performance:

Reading in Ginn 720 (*The Little Dog Laughed*). Child has memorized some words, such as *come*, *to*, *the*, *play*, but cannot recognize them if they are seen elsewhere.

Math is better; adds, subtracts simple problems.

Relevant personal information:

Child lives with mother and father—both are disabled—and the family receives public assistance. Both older siblings were in special day class (LH).

Parents come to school on a regular basis (about every 2 weeks). This is the only school student has attended. Note: Child is medicated for asthma and hay fever. His attendance has been good; 3 absences 1985–86 school year.

(Be sure to attach interventions log)

UNDERSTANDING PARENTAL FEELINGS

Upon learning that their child is having a problem at school, parents often show a variety of reactions. The reactions may or may not be voiced, and they vary in intensity among individuals. The amount of time it takes for parents to move from one stage to the next also varies, as follows:

1. Shock-denial. Parents want to gloss over the seriousness of the problem and say:
   "All kids fight."
   "I did that when I was a kid."
   "It's just a phase."

2. Anger-guilt-blaming. Parents admit that there is a problem but add:
   "It's all the teachers'/schools'/ex's fault."
   "If only I hadn't done . . . when I was pregnant."
   "What will people think?"
   "Why me? Is God punishing me?"

3. Resignation. Parents make remarks that include:
   "It's God's will."
   "Why not me? Bad luck can happen to anyone."
   (A support group, such as the Orton Dyslexia Society, can help at this stage.)

4. Depression. Some parents just become isolated, others call out for help and say:
   "I can't go on. What's the use?"
   (Counseling or medical intervention or parent support groups can help at this
   time.)

5. Acceptance. At this point, the family can function without being significantly distressed over the student's disability.

The Student Study Team process I am about to describe (see flowchart) often allays fears, removes guilt, and moves parents more quickly to the acceptance stage.

STUDENT STUDY TEAM PROCESS—FLOWCHART

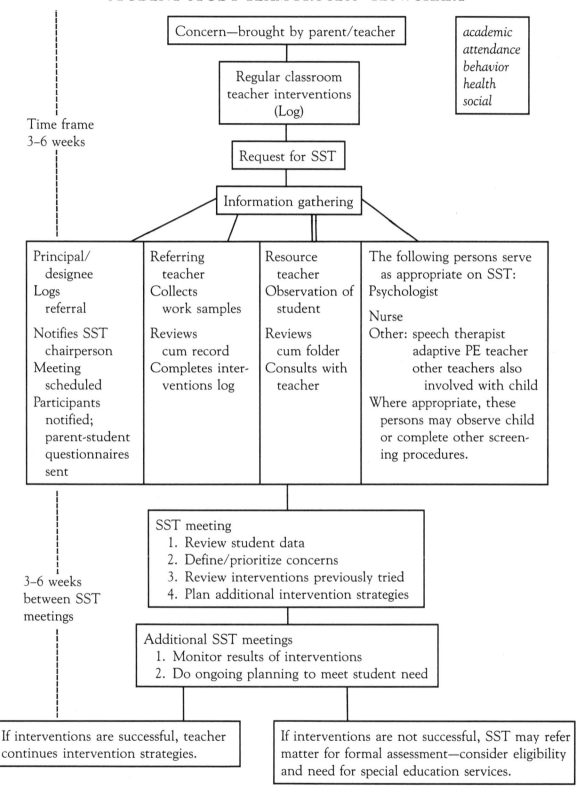

Concern—brought by parent/teacher

academic
attendance
behavior
health
social

Regular classroom teacher interventions (Log)

Time frame 3–6 weeks

Request for SST

Information gathering

Principal/ designee
Logs referral
Notifies SST chairperson
Meeting scheduled
Participants notified; parent-student questionnaires sent

Referring teacher
Collects work samples
Reviews cum record
Completes interventions log

Resource teacher
Observation of student
Reviews cum folder
Consults with teacher

The following persons serve as appropriate on SST:
Psychologist
Nurse
Other: speech therapist adaptive PE teacher other teachers also involved with child
Where appropriate, these persons may observe child or complete other screening procedures.

SST meeting
1. Review student data
2. Define/prioritize concerns
3. Review interventions previously tried
4. Plan additional intervention strategies

3–6 weeks between SST meetings

Additional SST meetings
1. Monitor results of interventions
2. Do ongoing planning to meet student need

If interventions are successful, teacher continues intervention strategies.

If interventions are not successful, SST may refer matter for formal assessment—consider eligibility and need for special education services.

STUDENT STUDY TEAM

The Student Study Team (SST) is an ideal forum for assisting students. Each school needs a sufficient number of SST teams to handle the requests in a reasonable period of time (3 weeks). (SST is a regular education function, designed to assist the regular class teacher meet student needs.)

A Student Study Team usually consists of the following persons:

1. Principal, or a designee, who generally acts as a facilitator
2. SST chairperson, who generally acts as a recorder
3. Referring teacher or classroom teacher
4. Resource teacher or resource specialist (RS)
5. Parents and student
6. Other personnel as appropriate; for example, psychologist, speech therapist, adaptive PE teacher, or nurse.

The SST chairperson schedules the meeting and notifies all participants.

Prior to the meeting, the referring teacher reviews the student's performance record and collects work samples. The resource teacher, psychologist, or resource specialist should have done at least one observation of the student—preferably in the area of the problem (this may be a subject area or may be an observation on the playground or in the cafeteria). This person should review the student's cum folder.

At my school, we have become convinced that when parents and the student are present at the meeting, we are more likely to resolve the problem in an effective way. Questions that arise can be answered immediately.

While we encourage parents to attend, sometimes they don't. It is advisable to hold the meeting anyway, hoping that the strategies developed will help.

The parent and student questionnaires that follow should be completed prior to the meeting. They may be mailed to the parents with a covering letter and a self-addressed stamped envelope for their return. If the parent does not attend the meeting, the questionnaires can be very helpful to the committee in its deliberations.

PARENT PREPARATION FOR SST

Note: Please complete this sheet and bring to the SST meeting.

1. Things I really enjoy about my child (his/her strengths) are:

   _____

   _____

2. Activities I think my child likes best are:

   _____

   _____

3. My concerns about my child are:

   a. At school

   _____

   _____

   b. At home

   _____

   _____

4. Types of discipline I find to be most effective with my child are:

   _____

   _____

5. Expectations I have for my child are:

   _____

Source: Marcie Radius, *Pat Lesniak Student Study Team Manual*, California Department of Education, 1987.

STUDENT WORKSHEET

1. At school, activities I really like are:

_____

2. The activities I like most away from school are:

_____

_____

3. The subjects I am best at are:

_____

_____

4. I learn best when: _____

_____

5. I want more help with these school subjects:

_____

6. If I could change one thing about school, it would be:

_____

7. My teacher, the principal, my parent(s), and I are having a meeting about me because:

_____

8. When I do things well, I like to do or get:

_____

9. When I grow up, I would like to be:

_____

At home:

1. My family (the people who live in my house) consists of:

_____

2. I get along best with:

_____

3. The person I like to talk to most is:

_____

Source: Marcie Radius, *Pat Lesniak Student Study Team Manual*, California Department of Education, 1987.

Student Study Team Process — Format for a Typical Meeting

The Student Study Team does the following:

1. Gathers student data.
2. Plans strategies to assist the student in the regular classroom.
3. Monitors student progress.

The Student Study Team is a group problem-solving process, with each member playing a role.

The role of the facilitator is to keep the team focused on the task and to see that all the members contribute their thoughts in an atmosphere that fosters trust. Trust occurs when each member of the team feels accepted and valued as a person and is involved and responsible for the outcome of the meeting. It is not desirable for one member to criticize or belittle another member, and the facilitator must intervene if this occurs. The facilitator must be sensitive to the feelings of each participant and see to it that each person gets to make a contribution. If one person is dominating the session, the facilitator again must intervene to ensure that everyone has been heard.

The role of the chairperson is to act as the recorder.

The semicircle provides a comfortable environment for the parent and student by focusing attention on the chart (not on them).

Visual memory sheet: 3' × 8' sheet of chart paper on which information is recorded. (See the format of that sheet.)

STUDENT STUDY TEAM SUMMARY

DATES OF MEETINGS

_____

_____

_____

_____

NAME OF STUDENT _____

TEACHER _____ SCHOOL _____ TEAM _____

STUDENT _____ PRIMARY LANG. _____ GR. ____ BIRTH ____ PARENTS ____

M ____ F ____

Strengths	Known Information	Modifications	Concerns (Prioritize)	Questions	Strategies Brainstorm	Actions (Prioritize)	Responsibility	
							Who?	When?

FOLLOW-UP DATE

Source: Marcie Radius, Pat Lesniak *Student Study Team Manual*, California Department of Education, 1987.

USE OF SST SUMMARY SHEET
(Typical Column Topics)

DATE OF MEETING _____ MEMBERS _____

TEACHER _____ SCHOOL _____ OF _____

STUDENT _____ PRIMARY LANG. _____ GR. _____ BIRTH _____ TEAM _____

M _____ F _____ PARENTS _____

Strengths	Information	Known Modifications	Concerns (Prioritized)	Questions	Strategies Brainstorm	Actions (Prioritized)	Persons Responsible Who?	When?
Academic Social Physical What student likes	School background Family composition Health Performance levels	Changes in program Reading specialist Tutoring Counseling Repeating grade	Academic Social/ emotional Physical Attendance	Questions that can't be answered at this time	Team brainstorms multiple creative strategies to address top concerns	Two to three actions chosen from strategies brainstormed	Any team member, including the parent and student	Specific dates

FOLLOW-UP DATE:
<u>(3-6 WEEKS)</u>

Source: Marcie Radius, *Pat Lesniak Student Study Team Manual*, California Department of Education, 1987.

The following is a list of the SST team members and a description of their roles:

1.   Facilitator (principal) greets and introduces the participants, states the purpose of the meeting; asks someone to act as timekeeper (15 minutes to cover strengths/ concerns/information; 15 additional minutes to brainstorm strategies and decide on a plan).

2.   Referring teacher leads off with a list of the student's strengths. (The committee tries to list 6 to 10 strengths. Of particular value is any statement that reflects on parenting, such as the student's good manners, neat appearance, or the parents' efforts to help the student. This seems to allay parental and student anxiety and sets a positive tone for the meeting.)

3.   Facilitator asks the parent or student to add to the list. A remark such as, "Is this *you?*" seems to relieve pressure.

4.   Referring teacher lists all concerns and prioritizes them.

5.   Recorder or any team member can ask for a clarification of concerns. For example, if absence is a problem, someone should ask, "Are absences for all day, or for a particular period?" If the complaint is that the student turns in little work, someone should clarify, "Is it a problem for all subjects?"

6.   Facilitator asks the parent or student to change anything or to add to the list.

7.   Information is entered: attendance records, grades, achievement scores, and so on. The referring teacher should be prepared to give this information. Enter all modifications that have been tried and give the results.

8.   Timekeeper calls time.

9.   Facilitator announces that the goal of the second half of the meeting is "to brainstorm strategies to help John," encouraging participants to list as many as they can in 3 to 4 minutes, not weighing their merit at this time.

10. Recorder records all suggestions. The following is a partial list to assist you:

Instructional Interventions

____ Change seating
____ Write directions
____ Limit number of directions
____ Use peer tutor, cross-age tutor
____ Test orally
____ Carrel out of traffic pattern
____ Shorter assignments
____ Student-teacher contract
____ Teacher help in prioritizing tasks to be done
____ Increase teacher-student time
____ Increase teacher-aide time

___ Remedial program within school
___ Remedial program outside school
___ Change materials (be specific)
___ Use additional learning approach
___ Allow to stay after school for extra help
___ Reward schedule (positive reinforcement)
___ Classroom change
___ Counseling
___ Provide immediate knowledge of results
___ Allow incomplete work to be done as homework
___ Parent to meet with teacher or resource specialist to learn techniques to help
___ Daily or weekly parent-teacher contact
___ Alternative assignments

11. Team members decide on 3 or 4 strategies to try for 3 to 6 weeks (being sensitive to the student's input and body language).

12. List who is responsible to carry out the strategy (can only be someone present at the meeting) and a date for doing it.

13. Follow-up meeting (3 to 6 weeks) is scheduled. This meeting will evaluate the results of the strategies.

14. Facilitator thanks the participants for coming.

15. Recorder transfers notes of the meeting to an 8½" × 11" Student Study Team Summary form, giving a copy to the parent, the principal, the referring teacher, and placing one in the student's cum folder.

16. Recorder rolls up and stores the visual memory chart until the follow-up meeting. When the follow-up meeting occurs, the original group memory sheet is again displayed. Reports of interventions are heard. At this time, the team can elect to continue with interventions or to move toward a formal assessment.

It is the intent of Public Law 94–142 that wherever possible students' needs should be met in the regular education program and that students should be referred for assessment and possible special education services only after the resources of the regular education program have been fully utilized and are clearly unable to meet their needs.

MULTIDISCIPLINARY PROCESS – FORMAL ASSESSMENT

Under the provisions of Public Law 94–142, assessment involves evaluation by a multi-disciplinary team: a psychologist, a nurse, a teacher with special training in learning problems, the regular class teacher, the parents, and a school administrator. The input of an occupational therapist, a physical therapist, or a speech therapist is solicited where appropriate. (See Referral Process flowchart.)

After gaining written permission for testing, there is a period of 50 days allowed for the completion of that assessment or within a period of 30 days after the start of the regular school year if the referral is made 20 days or less prior to the end of the school year—unless the parents agree, in writing, to an extension.

The psychologist gathers information regarding family history, social information, and cultural information from the parents. Information from an intellectual assessment or from adaptive behavior scales is also gathered to determine general ability level and to locate the child's strengths and weaknesses academically.

The specialist teacher generally helps with the academic assessment. Using various individualized tests, information is compiled about the child's reading, math, spelling, and writing skills. This person will also want to do several short observations of the student in the regular classroom.

Medical data and questions regarding the child's birth and early development are also part of the assessment. Generally the school nurse gathers this information by interviewing the parents. Simple tests to determine the child's ability to control motor functions are usually included, and the nurse should note any finding suggestive of deficits in central nervous system functioning. A cursory screening is done of the child's vision and hearing. Parents may elect to seek more thorough visual or audiological and pediatric examinations. It is helpful if they can obtain written reports and recommendations from physicians for the team's use.

When a student shows deficits in written or oral communication, the speech therapist's input is needed. When a student has an orthopedic or medical problem, the services of a physical therapist, an adaptive PE teacher, or an occupational therapist may be needed.

The classroom teacher who has worked with the child can provide valuable data regarding the child's motivation, frustration level, attention span, social acceptance, maturity, and emotional adjustment. Parents should be encouraged to take an active role in the evaluation process.

REFERRAL PROCESS—FLOWCHART

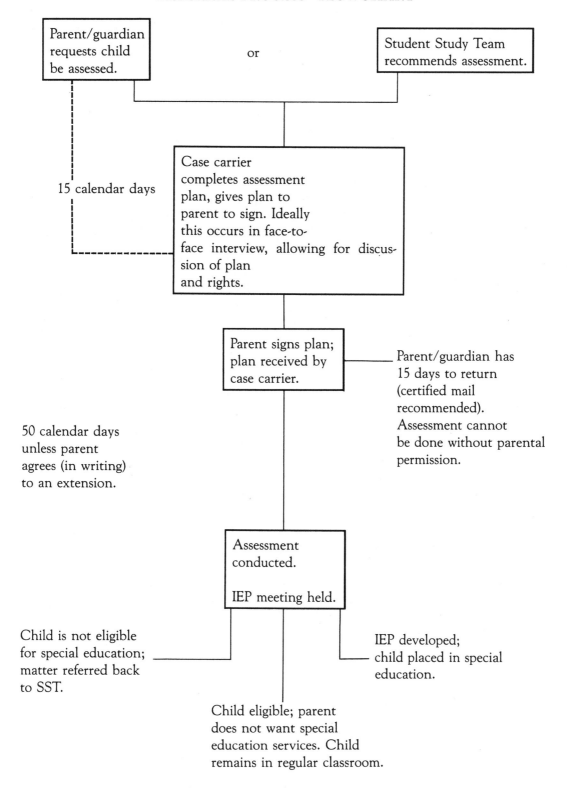

Parent/guardian requests child be assessed.

or

Student Study Team recommends assessment.

15 calendar days

Case carrier completes assessment plan, gives plan to parent to sign. Ideally this occurs in face-to-face interview, allowing for discussion of plan and rights.

Parent signs plan; plan received by case carrier.

Parent/guardian has 15 days to return (certified mail recommended). Assessment cannot be done without parental permission.

50 calendar days unless parent agrees (in writing) to an extension.

Assessment conducted.

IEP meeting held.

Child is not eligible for special education; matter referred back to SST.

IEP developed; child placed in special education.

Child eligible; parent does not want special education services. Child remains in regular classroom.

GUIDELINES FOR ASSESSMENT

Assessment includes both formal and informal procedures. In conducting an assessment, we must always remember that we are bound by legal and ethical considerations.

Legally, the following statements are true:

- Parental permission (written consent) must be obtained before the psychologist or special education personnel can administer any assessment device to the student.

- Parents have a right to an explanation of the types of assessments to be conducted (provided in their native language).

- Parents have a right to a copy of the findings of the assessment.

- Parents have a right to obtain an independent educational assessment and have the results be considered by the public agency.

- In the case of the bilingual child (a student who does not fluently speak English), we are legally bound to test the child in his native language by the use of an interpreter. In such cases, we must realize that the validity of the tests may be compromised.

Ethically, we must remember that we should be very careful about the words we use in our reports, and in talking about children. The purpose of our assessments is to help children. We want to concentrate our focus on how to use each student's strengths to greater advantage. While it is necessary to recognize a student's limitations, we want to seek ways to help students overcome or compensate for their areas of deficit.

> Tests are samples of behavior, and scores may be adversely affected by student anxiety and fatigue, or by emotional status. Since cooperation and motivation play such critical roles, we must not rely on test scores alone to assess a child's performance, but we must consider these test score results in relation to other indicators.

Intellectual Assessment

The psychologist may choose from a variety of devices to get a measure of the individual's intellectual functioning.[1] The instrument chosen should be appropriate to the age of the subject being tested and should be free of cultural bias. The following are commonly used tests. (As testing techniques advance, we may develop more definitive measures, so this list should not be considered unchangeable.)

---

[1]In some states, black children may not be given any intelligence test or parts thereof. Their intellectual functioning is gauged by their adaptive behaviors, personal history and development, classroom performance, and academic achievement.

Assessment Battery	Special Features
Woodcock-Johnson Psychoeducational Battery Tests of Cognitive Ability	age 4 to geriatric level
Wechsler Preschool and Primary Scale of Intelligence	children age 4–6½
McCarthy Scales	ages 2½–8½ years
Bender-Gestalt Test for Young Children	5–10 years old
Stanford Benet Intelligence Scale Form L-M	2–18
Wechsler Adult Intelligence Scale	16–75+
Leiter or the Columbia	used for testing children with communicative problems (limited English)
Wechsler Intelligence Scale for Children–Revised	age 6 to 16+

Known as the WISC-R, the Wechsler Intelligence Scale for Children-Revised is a popular and widely used device. It consists of 12 subtests, as follows:

Verbal Subtest	Measures
Information	Child's general fund of knowledge and alertness to everyday world
Vocabulary	Child's retrieval of information, abstract reasoning, quality of expression and thought
Comprehension	Child's common sense and social maturity (understanding of the rationale for rules)
Similarities	Child's memory (must hold 2 ideas in mind) and ability to think (compares 2 ideas for commonalities)
Arithmetic (timed)	Child's capacity to work under time pressure and ability to reason numerically
Digit span	Child's short-term memory

Performance Subtests	Measures
Picture completion	Awareness and memory of details
Picture arrangement	Understanding of causal relationships, sequential nature of events

Performance Subtests (cont.)	Measures (cont.)
Block design	Ability to perceive, analyze, and reproduce a design; measures visual-motor integration and manual coordination
Object assembly	Measures perceptual speed as child takes parts and unites them to form whole
Coding	Eye-hand control, motor speed, short-term visual memory, visual perception for directionality
Mazes	Measures figure-ground perception, attention, organization and planning, hand-eye coordination

The two profiles that follow may be helpful to you in understanding the scores obtained on a WISC-R:

Child A

Information	12	Picture completion	11
Similarities	10	Picture arrangement	10
Arithmetic	6	Block design	6
Vocabulary	13	Object assembly	10
Comprehension	11	Coding	5
Digit span	7	Mazes	not given

Verbal IQ   102   Performance IQ   88   Full Scale   95

The profile shown is rather typical of the learning-handicapped child. Its most obvious characteristic is the wide fluctuations in subtest scores. An average score is 10. On those tests where the child scored above 10, we are viewing the child's strengths. Scores below 10 reveal the child's weaknesses. Naturally, the lower the subtest scores and the greater the number of low scores, the more handicapped the child becomes. The child tested here fell within the range of average intelligence (IQ 90–110), but it is to be noted that because of the very low scores in the arithmetic area, this child is not likely to be doing well in the arithmetic portion of his regular classroom work.

Child B

Information	3	Picture completion	12
Similarities	3	Picture arrangement	8
Arithmetic	6	Block design	11
Vocabulary	5	Object assembly	11
Comprehension	5	Coding	11

Verbal IQ	66	Performance IQ	105	Full Scale	83

This child is going to need much help. He has a difficult time with language. When there is a discrepancy of 25 points or more between verbal and performance IQ (with Performance being higher), the child has a communicative disorder called *aphasia*. This child will need a lot of special help and support.

Academic Assessment

There are several quick and fairly reliable measurement devices commonly used. The following are being recommended because of the ease of administering them:[2]

Test and Appropriate Age	Measures
Wide Range Achievement Test (WRAT) Level I: 5–11 yrs. Level II: 12 yrs.–adulthood	arithmetic computational skills; spelling; ability to read words (does not measure comprehension of work meaning)
Peabody Individual Achievement Test (PIAT) Kindergarten to age 18	ability to understand math; ability to comprehend what is read; ability to choose correct spelling of a word from 4 choices; general information fund
Key Math Test Kindergarten to age 10	ability to reason mathematically without paper and pencil and with paper and pencil
Woodcock Reading Test Kindergarten to grade 12	measures ability to comprehend meaning, manipulate words in a variety of ways

---

[2]Other tests are available. See the list of sources of help at the end of this handbook for the names and publishers of tests.

You should give a minimum of at least two tests in each subject area—math, reading, and spelling. The testing sessions should not exceed one hour (less if the student shows excessive frustration or fatigue). Since student performance may vary day to day, it is wise to give only one complete test battery a day. By so doing, you have a better picture of the student's true performance. Monday is a poor day to test; likewise, any day following a holiday or preceding a holiday is a poor time.

The tests listed above are easy to give. *Read the test manuals carefully and completely before administering them.* If this is your first time to give these tests, and you can arrange for an experienced tester to observe your first try, that person will often be able to give you invaluable information regarding clues that can be picked up during testing. Look for clues such as the following:

1. How to evaluate the student's perceptual speed
2. How to probe for information in ways that will not invalidate your scores
3. How to read student body language
4. How to use information from the tests to prescribe (write goals)

The person who does the academic assessment will want to do the following:

1. Observe the student in class—4 observations of 10 minutes each. (It is suggested that you make two observations in the morning and two in the afternoon.)
2. Observe the student on the playground once; more than once if there is a behavioral problem involving the playground.
3. Obtain work samples, especially in the areas not covered by the tests just described—samples of student copying, student creative writing, and so on.
4. Interview the parents regarding their observations, expectations, and concerns.
5. Combine the findings into a written report. (See the following forms.)

Report of _____, Resource Specialist

_____
(date)

Student's name _____

Date of birth _____

Grade _____

I. Group test scores
    date   test results

II. Individualized Academic Tests
    date   test results

Statement re: Student performance during assessment

page 1 of __4__

Language assessment

    receptive—

    expressive—

    written (attach sample)—

Primary language _____

Perceptual assessment

    visual

    auditory

Motor assessment

    gross

    fine (attach sample)

Attention assessment

Cognitive assessment

Memory assessment

Social development

Medical and health findings

Recommendations

Observation record (attach additional pages as needed)

Report of _____ Joan M. Harwell _____ , Resource Specialist

———————————————
9/26/87
(date)

Student's name _____ Boy Young _____

Date of birth _____ 5/2/79 _____

Grade 1 (retained once in gr. 1)

I. Group test scores

date	test results
1986	scored below 1% in all areas

II. Individualized Academic Tests

date	test results				
5/1986	WRAT	Wd. Recog.	P1	SS	65
		Spell.	P1	SS	62
		Math.	1E	SS	88

date	test results	
5/1986	Woodcock Reading	Letter ID gr. 1.3
		Word ID gr. 1.2
		Wd. Attack—(knew 0) not able
		Wd. Comp.—0 to do any
		Passage 1.1

5/1986	Key Math	gr. 1.6

Statement re: Student performance during assessment

Boy is a very active, talkative, seven-year-old. During the PIAT, he appeared fascinated by the choice of answers. He often answered impulsively, but quickly changed his answer. In general, the final choice of answer was correct. He did show a number of reversals and sequencing; for example, *b/d*, *n/u*, *fit* for *ift*.

© 1989 by The Center for Applied Research in Education

Language assessment

receptive—Boy seems to have no problem processing info given at a normal pace in the 1:1 situation. In a group, however, he does not attend unless you are specifically talking to him. When given more than one direction at a time, he "forgets" all but the first one given.

expressive—Boy can express himself orally. His speech patterns contain phrases or short answers when he is questioned. He misarticulated several words, such as *chimney* (*chiminey*) and *spaghetti* (*sketti*).

written (attach sample)—Note: He could not spell last name correctly. He formed the *g* backward. He rotates paper when printing.

Primary language _____English_____

Perceptual assessment

visual Boy reverses *b/d* consistently, *p/q* occasionally. Inverts *n/u*, *m/w*. Does not distinguish between *h*, *r*, *n*.

auditory—Cannot discriminate short *e/i* sounds. Processing adequate 1:1, inadequate in group.

Motor assessment

gross—runs, skips, hops adequately.

fine (attach sample)—When cutting, the edges are not smooth. When coloring, he does not stay within boundaries. When gluing, he uses too much glue.

Attention assessment

Very distractible to sound and movement. Has some days that are better than others.

Cognitive assessment

On the Woodcock, Boy could not read any words, but when I gave the directions:

grass is to green as snow is to _____

one is to two as three is to _____

he is to she as boy is to _____

Boy had no difficulty seeing the relationship. On the Key Math Test, subsection missing elements, he was able to get questions 1 and 3 right.

Likewise, on the PIAT he could name *caboose* and tell that a sailboat moves because of the wind. His general informational fund was gr. 2.2.

Memory assessment

When asked to spell words he can read, such as *come, to, the, play*, he wrote *kum, ot, hte, pla*. When asked for his address and phone number, he had no difficulty giving them.

Social development

Boy takes responsibility for his daily hygiene. He appears neat and clean. His parents report that he does chores at home and usually completes the task.

He is impulsive. On the playground, his repeated aggressive acts have alienated him.

When asked what he'd like to be as a grown-up, he said he'd like to be in the army. He takes karate twice a week.

Medical and health findings

Child is on Dexedrine for hyperactivity. Parents administer this each morning. Previous trials with Cylert and Ritalin were not satisfactory.

At noon, Boy uses an asthma inhalant.

Recommendations

It is my impression that Boy would benefit from being in the resource specialist program. I believe that he needs a strong phonics-word attack approach.

Tests indicate that there is a discrepancy between his presumed ability (general knowledge fund 2.2) and his performance (essentially a nonreader).

Observation record (attach additional pages as needed)   Reading class, 10:00 A.M.

As I entered the room, Boy was talking with the boy sitting next to him. He watched as I spoke to his teacher. I sat several feet away from them. The teacher announced that I had come just to see what they were doing, so I circulated around the class looking at each student's paper.

Boy's task was to cut out 4 pictures and place them in sequential order. The paper attached is his product. The pictures were placed in sequence, but Boy had glue on his pants, the table, the scissors, and the floor. While carrying out this task, he talked nonstop to the boy next to him. He did not hear or did not respond when the teacher asked the students to clean up their work space. I noted that the interior of his desk was a mess.

PRIMARY LEARNING MODALITY
Observable Behaviors

Visual learner

___ Learns by seeing—watches to see what others do
___ Likes demonstrations
___ Recognizes words by sight—calls rabbit *bunny*, laugh *funny*
___ Often relies on initial consonants and configuration of words
___ Likes descriptions
___ Has lively imagination (daydreams, doodles), visualizes, thinks in color/pictures show much detail
___ Notices changes quickly
___ Notices color—movement (this can also be distracting)
___ Remembers faces more often than names
___ Takes notes
___ Has good handwriting
___ Tends to be very deliberate; plans in advance, organizes; thinks through problems
___ When in new situation, tends to be very quiet, observant
___ Is neat, meticulous
___ Prefers art to music
___ Sees detail or components (may miss seeing word or work as a whole)

Auditory learner

___ Loves noise/makes noise (may get in trouble for being noisy)
___ Enjoys talking, listening
___ When reading, vocalizes (moves lips, whispers, reads aloud to self)
___ Tends to use phonics
___ Remembers names more often than faces
___ Is receptive; expressive vocabularies are well developed for age (this can become a deficit if overtalks or does not listen during instruction)
___ Is easily distracted by sound
___ Talks problems out, tries out solutions verbally
___ Expresses emotion verbally (laughs out, shouts out)
___ Choice of clothing sometimes poor—no sense of what goes together
___ Prefers music to art

Kinesthetic (tactile) learner

___ Learns by doing, direct involvement (can be a deficit: often cannot mind own business)
___ Does not enjoy reading or being read to
___ Is poor speller
___ Has poor handwriting, especially when space becomes smaller. Often pushes too hard, no space between words
___ Images do not occur unless movement is involved
___ Does not attend to visual or auditory presentation
___ Fidgets, tinkers, touches, feels, manipulates; puts things in mouth
___ Is very physical with emotion (can be a problem: touching, standing too close, bothers others)
___ Reads laboriously
___ Has poor language development
___ Neither looks nor listens
___ Often seems absorbed by some inner life or thought—oblivious to surroundings

Learning Style Assessment

In recent years, educational research has suggested that most individuals have a preferred way to gain information (see the following form). The three common styles follow:

1. Visual learners rely primarily on vision for input—what they see, including written print. This group represents about 65 percent of the population.

2. Auditory learners gain most from what they hear. They love to talk and generally they listen attentively. This group contains about 15 percent of the population.

3. Tactile learners, or "tinkerers," learn by doing or by feeling, tasting, and touching. This group consists of perhaps 10 percent of the population.

Obviously these three groups do not account for 100 percent of all people. There are a few individuals who show no clearly preferred style.

Even though one modality may be preferred, good students use the other two modalities effectively. Learning-disabled students usually show deficits in one or more input channels or rely entirely on one channel.

While it would seem desirable to funnel all information through the preferred channel, we need to help students develop their other input channels in order for them to live richer lives.

In the one-to-one teaching situation, the most effective learning is done when you design lessons with the students' primary modality strength in mind. In the whole class situation, the most effective learning is accomplished when you design lessons to appeal to a variety of learners. For example, in science, the use of movies, slides, or closed circuit TV will appeal to the visual learners; tapes and discussions assist auditory learners; and guided experiments reach the tactile learners. The combination of all three approaches delivered to the whole group will benefit the majority of learners.

Health Assessment

The health assessment is an integral part of the evaluation. The assessment includes the taking of the child's medical history. The mother will be asked many questions regarding her pregnancy and delivery of this child, and additional questions regarding his early development and illnesses or accidents.

The health assessor (a physician or nurse) may then ask the student to perform some simple motor tasks.

At age 6 to 7, the child should be able to listen to 4 digits and repeat them accurately, to follow a series of 3 simple commands in correct order, to simultaneously open and close both hands (arms extended); to alternate left-right index finger to nose from arms extended; to do sequential finger opposition forward; to draw a round, closed circle, a square, and (while looking at a design) to copy a simple design such as

The child should not have to turn his head or the paper at odd angles to do so, and his tongue should not protrude while he performs the act. The child should be able to skip, stand on one foot with eyes open for 10 seconds, and build a 6-cube-tall block structure from 1-inch blocks. Older children should do these things and many more.

Ordinarily, the assessor will test the child's ability to read an eye chart on the wall and will check the child's general hearing acuity. The child's ability to visually track a moving object should be checked. The child's physical health is very important. A healthy child should have sufficient energy to do school activities. If significant findings occur, referral to a physician is in order.

The assessor should also look for eye preference, foot preference, and hand preference.

Social Assessment

An important aspect of assessment is that of the child's social adjustment. To get a true picture of a child's functioning, he needs to be observed in many different settings, at various times of day, and by more than one person.

Parents can provide enormous amounts of information about their child; it is to be remembered, however, that since children often behave differently with their parents than they do at school, it is equally important for the teacher to give her input.

We should ascertain whether the student grooms himself and does chores at home. We need to know what interests he pursues and to what degree. Does he have friends? Who? What age? What do they do together? We want to know if the child thinks of the future, and if so what his plans are for his life. What are his parents' expectations? Does the student have a regular homework routine—time and place? How does the parent get involved in that? Is he closer to one parent than to another? If there has been a divorce, how does he feel about that?

INDIVIDUAL EDUCATION PLAN

Following the assessment, the Individual Education Plan (IEP) team (a multidisciplinary team, principal, and child's teachers) meets with the parents to share the information gathered. If the student qualifies for special education services, the team may recommend that the child receive these services. *If the parent wishes the services*, an IEP will be developed. The team should be alert to parental wishes and careful to explain who will do what, when, and how.

Determining Appropriate Educational Setting

One of the most critical decisions to be made by the parent and the team is where the child's needs should be met—in the regular classroom, in a pull-out program for a few hours a day, or in a special class.

This decision is a personal one that weighs the student's strengths and academic functioning and the available resources of the school he attends, so explaining how this works is somewhat difficult because it varies from student to student and from school to school.

The law states that the student's needs should be met in the "least restrictive" environment able to meet his specific needs.

The following are ranked in order from least restrictive to most restrictive:

1. Regular class
2. Regular class with resource specialist support (up to one-half of the student's school day)
3. Special day class (SDC) (Students are in SDC at least 51 percent of the time up to 100% of the school day. This is the most restrictive setting on a regular school campus.)

For severely neurologically involved youngsters, or for emotionally disturbed youngsters, school districts may arrange for schooling in special schools or at special residential institutions, including hospitals or their home.

When a child is identified for the first time, generally the committee will suggest that the child remain in regular class with resource specialist assistance—either the resource specialist will come to the regular classroom to give help to the student or his teacher, or the student will go to the resource specialist's classroom for help with certain subjects (such as math or reading) while the student remains in regular class for other subjects (such as PE, music, art, science, or social studies).

If the student is not able to function adequately in any subject area offered in the regular classroom, he probably needs to be in special day class for most of the day.

Special day class students may be mainstreamed a period or two a day for subjects such as art, music, or PE. This decision requires much thought: Where is the student likely to make the maximum gains while having his self-esteem bolstered? If he is to remain in regular class, is the teacher willing to alter the way she works to accommodate the child's needs? For example, many children can pass social studies or science if the exam is given orally or if they are allowed to take an open-book test. It is probably unwise to place a student in a class where the receiving teacher actively opposes his placement. On the bright side, I have seen children with moderate learning disabilities function to their maximum potential in regular classrooms with sympathetic, empathetic, and flexible teachers.

Writing an Individual Education Plan

Once the educational setting has been determined, the educational goals should be developed. First, it must be determined whether the student will be given differential standards or be required to pass on regular standards. Each subject area needs to be considered. I am not sure how this works in other school districts, but I can state how it is working in mine. You will want to determine if this is consistent with practices in your district.

At the initial IEP team meeting, it is almost standard policy for us to give a student differential standards in one or more subjects since all students receiving special education assistance in our district are significantly behind academically. If the child meets the goals set by his IEP, he is then "promoted on differential standards." If he is also able to meet the standards for promotion set for all students by our board of education, he is "promoted on regular standards."

If, at the initial IEP team meeting or at some later date, it appears that the student is not going to be promoted because he has neither met the regular nor the differential standards, the IEP team will reconvene with the parents and make a recommendation, for example, that the student be "placed in the next grade" or be "retained in the present grade." If the committee recommends one thing and the parents insist on the other, we try to explain our position. If the parent continues to persist in a position not in concurrence with the team's recommendation, we do what the parent wants. A team report is generated showing (1) the team's recommendation and rationale; (2) the parents' decision; and (3) what will actually occur (the parents' wish).

Differential standards can be given in one subject only—for example, "math only," which means that the student must meet regular standards in all other areas. Or differential standards can be given in all subjects. It is not uncommon as a resource specialist to have students who are promoted on differential standards for a year or two and who then are able to catch up the third year and be able to be "promoted on regular standards" and exited from special education services.

If differential standards are given in a subject area, you must state what they are. Some possibilities include the following:

1. Extra time can be given to complete assignments and tests.

2. Tests may be read to students.

3. Students may respond orally instead of in writing; this may be very helpful in subjects such as science and social studies.

4. Tests may be administered in a quiet setting as opposed to in a group setting.

5. Students may use a textbook, calculator, tape recorder, or other devices to assist them.

6. The percentage required for passing may not be the same as the standard required of the regular class students.

7. Alternative tests may be given.

Next, educational goals are written for the student. You state which deficit areas the child will receive special assistance with. (See sample IEP, Part I and II at the end of this chapter and Part II in Chapter 5.)

The goals written do not represent the student's entire educational program. However, they should be extensive enough to ensure that the student will show steady growth toward his maximum potential and serve as a reminder to the teacher of essential learning needing to be covered.

DISSENTING OPINIONS

Occasionally, there is a disagreement regarding a child's needs. Persons not agreeing with the majority may register their objections by writing a dissenting opinion statement that is kept with the student's records.

DUE PROCESS

Parents and school districts have been involved in court cases to resolve issues that were not resolvable in the deliberations of the SST/IEP team process. Litigation is time-consuming, expensive, and unpleasant. Members of the Student Study Team and the multidisciplinary team should be certain that proper procedures are followed, that parental and student rights are protected, and that every effort is made to gain accord in the development of the IEP.

PARENTS' RIGHTS

It is a legal requirement that parents be given a copy of their rights. Due to limited space, the following is not a complete statement of parents' rights, but it is a statement of several very basic ones, among which are that the parents have the right:

1. to review and inspect all records;

2. to confidentiality—parents need to give written permission for the release of records or information to anyone (other agencies or physicians) other than themselves;

3. to request, when the information is no longer needed, that it be destroyed except for very basic information that might be needed later, for example, for social security benefits or for college admission as a special student;

4. to be notified in advance of meetings pertaining to their child and to have presentations made in that meeting in their native language;

5. to have their child tested in his native language;

6. to have an annual review of the child's educational program made by a team of people;

7. to bring someone of their choice to meetings to assist them;

8. to have the child educated in a program as close to home as possible;

9. to a series of services that include things such as transportation, counseling, medical services, which are written into the IEP and are free to the child and his family;

10. to participate in the development of the IEP;

11. to refer their own child for evaluation under Public Law 94–142 and to challenge the identification, placement, or education of their child; and

12. to prompt attention to their request.

ROLE OF CASE CARRIER IN MONITORING STUDENT PROGRESS

The case carrier has the responsibility to see that services are delivered in accordance with the intent of the IEP, to keep records showing the student's progress toward goals, and to retest yearly to ensure that the student is making progress and remains eligible for services. The case carrier meets with the parent and principal at least once a year to (1) review the student's progress, (2) write additional goals, and (3) complete necessary forms that certify the student remains eligible for special education services.

Every three years, the entire IEP team completely reassesses the student's progress, shares that information with the parent, and determines what continuing services, if any, are needed.

Sample of an Individual Education Plan

A sample IEP follows on pages 48–49.

INSTRUCTIONAL SETTING
☐SDC ■RSP ☐DIS ☐SS ☐NPS
☐H/H – ■EXTENDED YEAR

SAN BERNARDINO CITY UNIFIED
SPECIAL EDUCATION LOCAL PLAN AREA
INDIVIDUALIZED EDUCATION PROGRAM
Part I

DATE 3-7-89   INITIATION DATE 3-8-89

NEXT REVIEW DATE 3-90

THREE YEAR REVIEW DATE 3-92

MIS NUMBER |0|0|0|0|0|1|
(NUMBER)

NAME Doe, Jane   AKA
(LAST) (FIRST) (M)

almost
AGE 8.0 GRADE 2 (repeating)

BD 3-16-81 Name of ■Parent ☐Guardian ☐Foster Parent ☐Surrogate John Doe PHONE # none
(M/D/Y)

ADDRESS 1111 Favorite Street, Nowhere, Cal.
(NUMBER) (STREET) (CITY)

PROVISION FOR TRANSITION TO REGULAR CLASS

PROFICIENCY STANDARDS
☐ Regular Standards
■ Differential Standards

PROFICIENCY MET
Elementary ☐ Yes ■ No
Junior High ☐ Yes ■ No
Graduation ☐ Yes ☐ No

ALTERNATIVE MODE OF ADMINISTERING MINIMUM PROFICIENCY
☐ Simulated Perf ☐ Paper and Pencil Test
☐ Oral ☐ Braille ☐ Direct Performance
☐ Read Test to Student ■ Extended Time
■ Other 1:1 testing + 75% IEP obj

LANGUAGE
Home Lang. English
Student Lang. "
☐ FEP ☐ LEP

DESCRIPTION OF EDUCATIONAL PLACEMENT
Special Education Program 1-5 Hrs/Wk.
General Ed Program 25-30 Hrs/Wk.
Anticipated Duration 1 yr

Summary of Present Levels of Student Performance Areas

ACADEMIC SKILLS (Reading, Math, Spelling): PIAT 3-89 Math 3.2, RPI.8
R.C. 1.9 Spell. 2.0 Gen Info 2.9
Language, Communication: oral is adequate; written is poor
(omission of words, no space bet. wds.)

SELF-HELP SKILLS (Functional Skills, Independent Skills, Activities & Daily Living):
chores / child does w parental
grooming encouragement

PRE-VOCATIONAL & VOCATIONAL SKILLS (Awareness of Self, Exploratory Information, Work Experience):
little awareness, wants to be a
ballerina

SPECIAL ADAPTATION SKILLS (Cooperation, Attention, Organization, Social Acceptance, Responsibility):
parent is cooperative; student functions
best in 1:1 situation (free of distractions)

HEALTH-PHYSICAL DIAGNOSIS: ADD – Ritalin 5mg 2x/da.
Vision – hearing within normal limits
Rarely absent

PSYCHOMOTOR SKILLS (Auditory/Visual Perception, Fine/Gross Motor): Multiple visual
perceptual deficits (b/d reversals, sequencing
and memory deficits)
PHYSICAL SKILLS (motor performance, fitness): Gross – ok Fine – poor

OTHER:

PARENT APPROVAL
My signature indicates that I consent to the Individualized Education Program placement, and my rights to appeal have been explained to me.

X _John Doe_
Signature of Parent   3-7-89
M/D/Y

_____
Signature of Pupil   M/D/Y

PHYSICAL EDUCATION
■ Reg. PE
☐ Ad or Md PE - Reg. Program
☐ PE in Spec. Set.

DESIGNATED INSTRUCTION
☐ APE
☐ Speech Therapy
☐ Other
☐ Other
☐ Other

☐ Special Transportation

☐ Dissenting Opinion

ANNUAL GOALS
Student will show improvement in:
- lang. arts
- reading

PARENT CONTACT for IEP CONFERENCE		APPROVAL DATE	
2-22-89 letter		_Sally Nice_	3-7-89
M/D/Y Method		Special Ed Teacher	M/D/Y
3-1-88 personal contact		_Mrs. J. Stern_	3-7-89
M/D/Y Method		Regular Ed Teacher	M/D/Y
		Admin	3-7-89
		Administrator	M/D/Y
3-6-88 note		S. Binet - Psych	3-7-89
M/D/Y Method		Other – Specify	M/D/Y
		Betta Dunn RN	3-7-89
M/D/Y Method		Other – Specify	M/D/Y

White – Program Supervisor or District Office   Canary - Teacher   Pink – Parent   Goldenrod – Cum File

SE-50 (Rev: 7/87)

48

SAN BERNARDINO CITY UNIFIED SPECIAL EDUCATION LOCAL PLAN AREA

INDIVIDUALIZED EDUCATION PROGRAM — PART II

NAME _Doe, Jane_

BIRTHDATE _3-16-81_

DATE _3-7-89_

sample form

Short Term Objectives	Person(s) Responsible For Implementation *	Hours Per Week **	Methods, Materials and Activities	Evaluation
By: _(date)_ the student will demonstrate an increased competency in: GOAL — _skill area_ OBJ: _(name of student)_ will _(what/how)_ To _(what degree of accuracy)_	_who_		_how often will skill be practiced_ _what materials and activities will be used_	Achieved ___ Not Achieved _1_ METHODS OF MEASUREMENT ☐ Observer ☐ Teacher Made Test ☐ Standardized Test ☐ CR Test ☐ Other
By: _5-31-89_ the student will demonstrate an increased competency in: GOAL — _alphabetizing_ OBJ: _Jane will alphabetize by first letter 10 lists of 5 words each she will make 100% on 8 out of 10 lists_	_Rap_	_15min_	_2 - 3 x weekly_ _practice using words familiar to her or decodable_	Achieved ___ Not Achieved ___ METHODS OF MEASUREMENT ☐ Observer ☒ Teacher Made Test ☐ Standardized Test ☐ CR Test ☐ Other
By: _9-28-90_ the student will demonstrate an increased competency in: GOAL — _alphabetizing_ OBJ: _Jane will alphabetize by first + second letter 10 lists of 8 wds each making 100% on 8 out of 10 lists_	_Rap_	_15min_	✓	Achieved ___ Not Achieved ___ METHODS OF MEASUREMENT ☐ Observer ☒ Teacher Made Test ☐ Standardized Test ☐ CR Test ☐ Other
By: _____ the student will demonstrate an increased competency in: GOAL — OBJ: _(See Chapter II for a full blown IEP PtII)_	*	**		Achieved ___ Not Achieved ___ METHODS OF MEASUREMENT ☐ Observer ☐ Teacher Made Test ☐ Standardized Test ☐ CR Test ☐ Other
By: _____ the student will demonstrate an increased competency in: GOAL — OBJ:	*	**		Achieved ___ Not Achieved ___ METHODS OF MEASUREMENT ☐ Observer ☐ Teacher Made Test ☐ Standardized Test ☐ CR Test ☐ Other

SE-51 (Rev. 7/87)   This is not a contract for services   White — Program Supervisor or District Office   Canary — Teacher   Pink — Parent   Goldenrod — Cum File   Circle all revisions of IEP with date and parent, teacher and administrator's initials

49

3

CLASSROOM MANAGEMENT

A teacher makes hundreds of decisions every day—decisions while planning and on-the-spot decisions—while carrying out each day's activities. The importance of careful planning cannot be underestimated. Teachers who preplan do a more effective job than they would do if they didn't preplan. The questions posed in this chapter reflect questions that teachers have asked me over the years.

ENVIRONMENTAL DECISIONS

How to Create a Utilitarian and Attractive Classroom

1. Begin with a clean, well-organized room.

2. Arrange desks so that you and the chalkboard are focal points. One of the following arrangements may suit you:

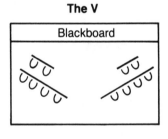

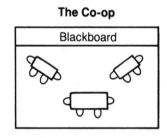

3. Decorate with plants, mobiles, student art work, a learning center, and a reader's corner with magazines and appropriate books. Bulletin boards that can be used all year by merely changing a few displays are time-savers. One such board can be used all year to display good papers, as follows:

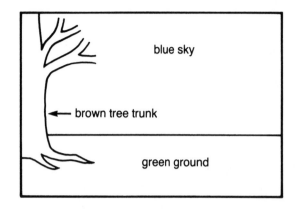

September—green leaves, apples, a school house

October—multicolored leaves, a haystack, pumpkins and fence

November—brown leaves on the green ground; Pilgrims

December—bare tree (change the green ground to white), snowman

4. Obtain essential equipment, such as paper, pencils, scissors, glue, crayons, and chalk; chart paper (handy for preserving and displaying information that has on-going value); and texts

BEHAVIORAL MANAGEMENT CONSIDERATIONS

First Week Activities

Plan your first day and first week carefully. It is better to err in favor of too many activities than too few. The best activities to choose are:

1. relatively short;

2. require few directions—little or no new teaching (for example, review nature);

3. allow you to be free to move around, get to know students, solve problems, give positive feedback;

4. allow students to be successful; and

5. build a feeling of belonging to the group.

The following are some suggested activities:

1. Make Polaroid pictures of each student to display.

2. Choose a class name.

3. Introduce a classmate to the group: Pair off, give a list of questions to ask; they interview each other for 5 minutes, then introduce each other to the group. For this to be successful, students must have questions they will ask each other, and there must be a payoff for a good job (recess time, an edible for a nice job).

4. Keep files of puzzles, word searches, art activity, musical activity.

5. Check with the principal or resource specialist to see whether you need to give reading or math placement tests.

Establishing Rules

1. Have rules posted in at least two locations. Some suggested rules are as follows:

---

1. Complete Your Own Work.

2. Let Others Work. Let Your Teacher Teach.

3. Be Kind. Respect Others and Their Property.

---

2. During the first week, teach students the following:

What the rules mean

How to act in acceptable ways—role-play/model

What the consequences will be when a rule is broken

How to immediately become quiet upon a signal (the peace sign works well)

During the first week of school, plan your lessons so that you can watch for and handle violations of the rules as they occur. When a student violates a rule, take her to the rule board (rules should be posted), tell her what she did to violate the rule, and suggest to her another way of handling the situation. Sometimes you may wish to stop the class and then "replay" the conditions at the time of the infraction so that the offender can practice the new way to handle the situation. This allows other class members to benefit from her experience.

In handling first-week violations, be kind but firm about what you expect. For example, if a student is out of her seat at an inappropriate time, say, "Mary, I'm sorry. You may not leave your desk now. That disturbs me [point to rule 2]. Raise your hand and wait, please." Have students help Mary replay the circumstances so that she can practice the new behavior.

I have found that limiting movement in the room increases the likelihood of on-task behavior. A class monitor can be helpful. That person can sharpen a pencil or obtain an item for a student. (Monitor responsibility should be rotated among all the students.)

During the first week, when students do raise their hands, recognize them quickly. If the request was for something you'd like to discourage, make a note and talk to the student in private, quietly, gently but firmly, about how you'd like her to handle that in the future.

After the first week, you must consistently enforce logical consequences for the violation of rules. A logical consequence for violation of rule 1, "Complete Your Own Work," would involve working out a way to get the work done—(for example, loss of recess, homework plan agreed to by parent, time after school, loss of a desired privilege until the work is done).

Students should be held responsible for work production. To fail to do so will cause unbelievable difficulties for all concerned. There are two pitfalls to avoid: (1) if the student fails to do the original assignment, don't double it! and (2) talk with the student in private to ascertain why it was not done. Should you determine that she doesn't know how, substitute a different (perhaps easier) assignment—one that she can do—or teach her how to do the things she couldn't do. If it is a student with severe attention deficits, you may want to agree to accept portions of the assignment until it's all done and to give slightly shorter future assignments.

Logical consequences for rule 2, "Let Others Work. Let Your Teacher Teach," might include a warning for the first offense, a time-out for the second offense, and an isolation for the third offense, as follows:

1. Warning. "Mary, this is a warning. Work without talking, please."

2. Time-out. "Mary, go to the time-out corner." In time-out, the student is excluded from group activity but can still see what is going on. She writes, "I will be quiet so that others can work" five times. If Mary has gone to time-out satisfactorily and does her sentences quietly, she can return to the group at the end of the time it takes to write the sentences. Time spent in time-out must be made up before school or at recess.

3. Isolation. If Mary is talkative or noisy or returns from time-out and commits another offense within the same instructional period, an isolation option is used. The student is removed from the room and goes to the nurse's office, to the counselor or administrator's office, or to another teacher's classroom for a set amount of time, generally until the end of the period. All time spent in isolation must be made up.

In both time-out and isolation, the student should not be left alone. Her activities should be monitored by some legally responsible adult.

Records must be kept. At the end of the day, the teacher's log on each student should reflect the offense, the method of handling, and the results. Students need to understand that isolation results in loss of the class's next major privilege (a movie, a dance, or a field trip). Two isolations in a five-day period will result in a letter sent home to the parents.

It is understood that if a student is placed in time-out, then isolation, then returns to class the next period and continues to be a disturbance, she will be excluded from the classroom for the rest of the day. The administrator should decide whether the student will be allowed to remain at school or will be sent home, but the student may not return to her own classroom—even if she is contrite—for that day.

The time-out and isolation options have been shown by research to be effective in reducing behaviors such as talking, profanity, inappropriate out-of-seat behaviors, tantrums, and aggressive behaviors. Consistency, fairness, and administrative support of the policy is critical to its success. It is wise to explain your system and to ascertain that you have that support.

Creating Positive Feeling Tone

Research has shown that the single most important variable in learning is the teacher-pupil relationship. Students work harder for a teacher they like. What are the characteristics they like? Ask them, and they may say one of the following:

"Fair."

"Pleasant."

"Doesn't yell."

"Talks to us. Lets us give our opinions."

"Gives us rewards for good work."

"Cares how I feel."

"Reads to us."

"Acts as if she likes us."

"Doesn't let us act bad."

"Doesn't preach. Listens to us."

Successful teachers seem to have one common denominator: They take time to communicate individually on a personal level with students. The more relaxed types do it during class; the more organized types do it during conference periods or before and after class. In the classroom, they do not scream—they are clearly in control, as shown by a high degree of on-task behavior. There is an absence of behavioral problems and quiet handling of potentially disruptive situations. Their tone of voice implies friendliness and caring.

Finding Better Ways to Talk to Children

When we talk to children, we should do the following:

1. Show respect for the student.
2. Make our expectations clear.
3. Reflect a sense of humor.
4. Get students to do what we want them to do.

I am reminded of a story related to me by an LD adult. She was talking about an experience she had had in the fourth grade. Being mentally gifted, she was able to maintain her grades without any assistance from special education, but there were areas of the curriculum (such as math) that she found troublesome. She learned to hate school and refused to work in order to go to college—primarily due to a fourth grade teacher's poor handling of a situation.

It seems that the teacher had introduced a new concept that day—gravity. He had talked about it for some time. This woman said that she was usually not a good listener, but that on this particular day she had been diligently listening, enthralled with the idea that this mysterious force was keeping her on planet Earth. She wanted to know more, but she was too timid to raise her hand because she did not like to call attention to herself. (LD children believe that they are dumb and that by remaining quiet no one will know it.) Finally she gathered up all her courage, raised her hand, and asked, "Mr. Jones, what *is* gravity?"

The teacher could have dignified her response by saying, "I know it's hard to understand. Like electricity, you can't see it, but it's there." Instead, he replied, "I've been talking about this for an hour. Where have you been, girl?" She told me that that was the last time she ever asked a question in school.

It is easy to lose patience, but when we do so—even once—we can cause irreparable damage (as it did in this case). Students relate cooperatively to teachers who show respect for them.

Teachers who are good communicators send clear messages. In one classroom I observed, the teacher told the students that they could not go to lunch until the floor was clean. The students picked up the papers and were frustrated when she kept saying, "The floor is still dirty." Finally one angry student said, "What's wrong with it?" She said, "I want those sunflower seed shells picked up, too." At that point, the students understood, and they quickly complied with her request.

Another example occurred in the hallway. A teacher was berating upper-grade students for "walking like kindergarteners." As she did so, they exaggerated their poor behavior to live up to her statement. Another teacher said, "Stop." The students did. Then she said, "I'd really appreciate it if you'd walk quietly, and without touching others." They did.

A sense of humor can also be very handy. To illustrate, a student who is rocking in her chair is in danger of toppling over. Instead of yelling, "Put all the legs of that chair on the floor!" the teacher said, "You're in grave danger, Mary. Chairs are not inanimate objects. They sit around thinking up ways to hurt people. If that one is allowed to get its way, you're going to end up with a split chin or a large bump on your head. Who is going to win—you or that chair?" Mary responded by putting the chair legs on the floor.

One day I overheard my tutor trying to deal with a very obstreperous sixth grade youngster. His assignment was to do some math problems and then to write some sentences. She asked him which task he wanted to do first. He chose the sentences. When he wrote the first sentence, it contained three words. She read his body language: As he finished it, he rocked his chair back on its hind legs (defiance) and folded his arms (not open to instruction). He was poised for the criticism he expected would follow.

She looked at him and said, "You really did a nice job of making that *t*. It's nice and tall and you remembered to cross it. Leave a couple of lines between this sentence and the next one. That will make your work look nice."

He wrote the second sentence—again, only three words. His body language still said, "I'm angry. You can't make me do anything I don't want to." She said, "You certainly do understand about nouns and verbs. Good. Very good." Again she asked him to leave some space.

In the third sentence, he wrote five or six words and said, "I know about phrases, too." She said, "You obviously do. Could you add a phrase or two to your first two sentences?" He did. She said, "Wow! Your sentences are just great!" By now the student was much more relaxed and obviously feeling better. He was now open to instruction.

The tutor had used her head. By reading his body language, she knew that she should avoid a confrontational situation with him. She gave him some control over making a choice and seemingly accepted his work. Her careful scrutiny of his work allowed her to find something legitimate to compliment.

Children provide teachers with many challenges. Because they are young, they often do things without considering the consequences. Some teachers sound like drill sergeants. They extract better behavior from children through fear of reprisal. Other teachers can get the same improvement in behavior through the use of more pleasant techniques.

The following are some examples:

Poor: You want to talk. Then you get up and teach this class.

Better: Mary, could you let me finish this, and then we'll hear what you want to add to help us understand the lesson. Listen closely so that you are sure of what you want to say.

Poor: Stop running in the hall! Go back and walk!

Better: Walk, please. [If you are dealing with a repeat offender, have her come in at recess or lunch to practice walking when she has no audience to perform for.]

Poor: Your mouth runs all the time!

Better: [In private, develop a contract that you and the student write out and sign. The contract should state the number of quiet minutes earned and name the privilege or reward. The contract should also state that failure to be quiet will result in a specified punishment.]

Poor: You've both got detention. There will be no fighting when I'm around.

Better: Come sit with me and tell me about your disagreement. Maybe we can find a solution. [About half of all fights result from misunderstandings. Talking it out teaches students to be less combative in the future.]

Poor: You won't do your work? Of course, you'll do your work or I'll punish you.

Better: Let me sit down and you can tell me why you feel that way. Maybe I gave you work that is too hard. [They'll deny that it's too hard. You say, "I'm afraid it's too hard for you. If not, show me."]

Poor: Mary, do your work and stop acting as if you're stupid.

Better: I am sure you know how to do this. What's the matter?

Poor: That's wrong!

Better: I'm not sure I understand what you mean. Can you tell me more?

Students are more likely to respond in the ways we want them to if they are treated with dignity and respect.

Providing Alternatives for Faster Students

Within any classroom, you will find that you have students who work at various paces. Generally it follows a bell curve, as in the following example:

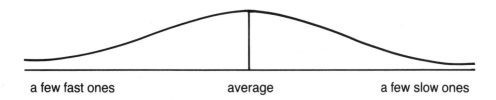

a few fast ones   average   a few slow ones

The problem is to find ways to handle this without being viewed as unfair. This makes for a good early discussion topic. You can ask for students' input: "Should I give the same work to everybody?" At first, they'll usually say, "Yes." You say, "Oh, at about 11:30 I'm going to put a hundred multiplication problems on the board. You can't go to lunch until they're done and corrected." Someone will say, "What if we don't know how?" You answer, "Tough." Give them time to digest your answer, then say, "Would that be fair?" Usually they see that it isn't.

Early in the year, they should see their Individual Education Plans. If you take some time to help them to see what they must do, they will realize that they have different requirements to meet. After a week or two, you'll know enough about your students to group them for instruction.

"*What do you do with students who work fast?*" They can act as coaches or clerks. They can be trained to help others or to grade papers. Sometimes they can help in another classroom, in the cafeteria, or in the office.

The following are other suggestions:

1. Establish a listening center and have tapes that are interesting. Oddly enough, tapes of their social studies or science texts are often voluntarily chosen.

2. Establish a center with art materials that can be used quickly (colored pencils, colored chalk and fixer, modeling clay, tracing activities, glue, and scissors).

3. Allow fast students to read to average students or vice versa. A daily newspaper and age-appropriate magazines should be available. (*National Geographic* magazine is full of wonderful pictures and information that students find interesting.)

4. Encourage fast students to do their homework in class. Be sure to give them a note to take home so that parents will know it was done.

5. Grant extra credit for extra assignments. However, do not *force* a fast student to do extra work.

Providing Alternatives for Slower Students

When planning assignments, it is good to look over your class roll to anticipate who will have trouble doing them. Who cannot do this? How shall I provide for these students' needs?

The following are some of the methods available:

1. Give slower students a different assignment (lower level of difficulty).

2. Shorten the assignment for some students (choose only the most important items or pages).

3. Allow more time to complete the task.

4. Allow for the use of "crutches" or "bypass" techniques (calculators, multiplication tables, or typewriters).

5. Allow extra help from a study-buddy, in a cooperative learning group, or from a teacher aide.

6. Place students in a slower-paced group.

7. Allow for alternative responses. Some answers could be given orally—eliminating tedious writing.

8. Reproduce material instead of requiring students to copy it (as in the case of math pages) or allow them to write only the answers.

9. When the student's main problem is reading, highlight the important part of the text (critical ideas in red, key vocabulary in green, specific names and events in blue). Read along with them—choral reading can be very effective.

10. Help the student get organized. Help her to decide which assignment to do first, to clear her desk so that only that assignment is on top, to set a timer so that she can pace herself.

11. Provide continued practice until the skill feels comfortable:

    a. Show her how.
    b. Watch her do the process, coaching if she gets stuck.
    c. Give sufficient daily practice for enough days to be certain that the skill is mastered before testing.

    Open-book, multiple-choice, and true or false tests may be given before recall tests in subjects such as social studies and science.

12. Allow for demonstrations and projects where appropriate as testing devices.

Preventing Misbehavior

Students who show a high degree of on-task behavior do not have time for misbehavior. To be on-task, students must be placed in appropriate materials, be in appropriate groups for instructions, and receive quick attention if they are having trouble.

How do I determine what are appropriate materials? Appropriate materials are materials that the student can do successfully with only a little help. The materials should be attractive and appropriate to the student's age, interests, and ability. The Key Math Test and the Woodcock Reading Test are particularly helpful in locating the student's functioning level. A cardinal rule given to me by a professor stated: "Start low, go slow!" For example, scan a student's profile on the Woodcock. If she is to read silently, selections must be at her easy reading level. If she is to be working with you, assign her to her reading grade level. Under no circumstances should a child be asked to read at her failure reading level. Consult the Woodcock profile to determine where these levels are.

The Key Math Test also gives a grade level score. If a student showed a grade score of 4.3, I would start her at the beginning of grade 4 material. If her score was 4.8, I might start her in grade 5 material, but only if I could see my way clear to giving her lots of help. It is imperative for such a student to be in a small group and to get help from me or from the teacher assistant.

"How do I decide on an appropriate group?" Misbehavior is more likely to occur as groups get bigger—groups of four or fewer seem to work better for LD students. There are some

students who are so volatile that they cannot work in a group and need one-to-one instruction. If a student is having difficulty—academically or behaviorally—we want to be sure that she is in the most appropriate group for instruction. She may need to be with other children. A volatile child can disturb a whole group. You may need to experiment a bit to find a group where she demonstrates that she can work. If such a group does not exist in your room, perhaps she needs to go to another teacher's room for a part of the day.

As a resource specialist, serving children of all ages, I find that in my situation I sometimes do better to group students by personality rather than by subject or grade level. It is not unusual for me to have two second graders working in a group with two fourth graders. The grouping looks like this:

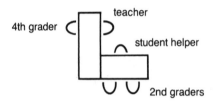

Sometimes one of the fourth graders will be listening to the second graders read while I give extra help to the other fourth grader. Sometimes the fourth graders are working in workbooks while I'm instructing the second graders.

The proximity of an adult to students who are having academic or social difficulty is of utmost value. A touch of your hand on the shoulder or a look is often all that is needed to head off a potential problem. A classroom aide, a parent helper, or a cross-age tutor can be a great asset since all students can then be near an older person. Generally the worst offender needs to be closest to you. Adult helpers don't necessarily have to teach. They can help by just sitting near the volatile student and talking with her until you're available.

Value of Positive and Negative Reinforcers and the Use of Extinction

For most special education students, there must be a payoff for work done. By using a skillful combination of positive and negative reinforcers and extinction, successful teachers obtain the behaviors they want.

Positive reinforcers are extrinsic or intrinsic rewards that stimulate children to put forth better effort. Extrinsic reinforcers are tangible rewards given to students, such as edibles, toys, useful items (pencils, notebooks), stickers, or special privileges and certificates. As children develop more positive self-esteem, they begin to work for more intrinsic rewards such as verbal praise from parents or teachers, seeing their improvement on progress charts, and getting good grades.

Not all children respond to the same type of reward. At the beginning of the year, you might want to talk to students and note their individual preferences as to the type of reward they prefer.

Negative reinforcers are the consequences that befall a student when she fails to put forth effort. An effective negative reinforcer is one that motivates the student to alter her behavior or performance. Negative reinforcers include deprivation of privileges, writing sentences, poor work notices or grades, or punishment, such as time-out, isolation, or detention.

Extinction occurs when an undesirable behavior disappears. There are occasional behaviors, such as tattling, that may disappear simply by ignoring them. However, if you ignore them in one student and punish the same offense in another, you will lose credibility and may be deemed unfair.

Four Types of Difficult Students

The following chart may help you identify and work more successfully with difficult students:

Attention seekers—operate from a faulty belief: for example, "I belong only when I am being noticed."

____ quarrel with peers

____ make excessive noise (tapping, moving chair, slamming books, rattling paper)

____ tattler

____ teller of wild tales

____ excessive talker

____ out of seat

____ tardy frequently, coupled with loud arrival

____ make mouth noises (whistles, hums, and so on)

____ fretful, whine, pout

____ baby talk

____ throw things/tantrums

Dependents—operate from the belief that they are helpless: for example, "Oh, well, it's just my lot in life. I have no clout. I'm helpless and powerless."

____ feel dumb

____ withdraw

____ say, "I can't do it" frequently

____ won't try

____ give up easily

____ inept

____ cry often

____ fearful or panicky

____ frequently says that they're ill

____ want to be left alone

____ cling to adults

____ helpless

____ poor achievers

Power seekers—operate from a faulty belief: for example, "I must be the boss. No one can boss me."

___ defiant	___ stubborn
___ must be right/argue	___ must be "first," get angry if they are not
___ very aggressive (bossy/bully)	
___ rebel	___ dawdle (passive aggression)
___ manipulate peers	___ talk back
___ manipulate adults	___ rigid
___ put others down	___ have few friends
___ perfectionist	___ truant
___ lie	

Revenge seekers—operate from the belief that the world is a hostile place; no one can be trusted; they cannot be loved.

___ aggressive physically (bite, fight, throw rocks)	___ loner
	___ not liked by anyone
___ sarcastic/negative	___ set fires
___ destroy property	___ start false rumors
___ cheat, steal, ignore/put down others/name callers	___ distrust others

Attention seekers.   Find out whose attention they want, and let them know that you will help them find ways to get it. You can work this out by talking in private.

Dependents.   (See the section on failure syndrome in Chapter 4.) Allow children to be increasingly successful. Praise, good notes, and time with teacher are rewards preferred by these students.

Power seekers.   Recognize that these students are feeling powerless and insecure. Offer them choices as to the type of assignment or the order in which they do assignments.
Avoid a confrontational situation, if you can. If you must deal with an issue, do so where other students cannot hear (preferably with another adult present as a witness). Power seekers respond well to consistency, fairness, and contracts with payoffs. Sometimes you can get power seekers to change their orientation. Usually they need to deal with their true feelings of being victims. At first, they'll require a lot of help to take more constructive action.

Revenge seekers.   Revenge-seeking students often rate high in the power-seeking category as well. Give them choices and contracts with payoffs. They feel like victims and are determined to get even. The prognosis for revenge seekers is poor. Long-term therapy is generally needed. Revenge seekers don't seek therapy because they do not see themselves as part of the problem. They believe that their difficulties are caused by others. Many are products of dysfunctional homes where the parents are character-disordered. Such students are amoral and asocial. Their inappropriate attitudes have been internalized during their formative years. The prognosis for these students is poor since their inappropriateness is often reinforced at home. Rewards are often ineffective because such students are getting status and attention because of their behavior. (A significant number of these children have an attentional deficit and benefit from drug therapy. That avenue of help should be explored.)

Handling Misbehavior

We teachers often see behaviors that are bothersome: for example, a student kicks a classmate, destroys her paper or pencil, steals, and so on. The key to dealing with these behaviors is asking the student why she did what she did. We cannot work on solutions until the student tells us why she acts in a particular way. For example, when a student tears up her paper, was it because of the following:

1. She didn't know how to do the work?

2. She is too critical of her own work?

3. She was angry—if so, at whom and why?

Once the "why" is isolated, possible solutions can be generated, discussed, and tried.

Since finding out why a student does something may be time-consuming, this should be done in private so as not to take up precious instructional time.

From time to time, we must deal with misbehaving students under circumstances where time-out or isolation is not an available alternative.

In these situations, the most effective technique I have found is this. Get very near such a student, establish eye contact, and quietly say, "Your behavior is inappropriate. Can you fix it?" When she does, I say, "Thank you."

MANAGEMENT: CRISIS INTERVENTION

In dealing with a student who is exhibiting violent or aggressive behavior, teachers should be aware of these guidelines:

1. Never grab or touch an acting out or violent student unless he is causing harm to another person or himself.

2. Send for assistance. (If possible, always wait for help if you intend to become physically involved.)

3. If student is threatening, keep a normal distance from him. Do not invade his space.

4. Keep your voice tone normal. Repeat any instructions until the student complies. (Try to remain calm.) If a student is violent or about to hurt another, yell "stop" and the student's name, then lower your voice. Screaming many words or threatening only confuses or further elevates the student's activity level.

5. Immediately try to get the aggressive student into isolation where he can calm down. Talk to him in a low, calm voice or remain silent.

6. Do not leave the student alone until he visibly calms down. (You might have another adult stay with him if you cannot.)

7. Discuss his behavior and the consequences of his behavior only after he has become calm.

(From "Crisis Management Workshop," 1983. Permission granted by authors, Crane-Reynold, Inc., 9327 A Katy Freeway, Suite 327, Houston, TX 77024, 713-984-0688.)

"What do you do when all else you've done fails?" Once in a while, you will encounter a student who does not adjust. You cannot allow a recalcitrant student to destroy the group. Misbehavior is contagious. The student should be removed from that classroom but be given a chance in another classroom or school. If that does not work, she may need a shorter day or a more restrictive environment. The possibility of an attention deficit disorder should be explored. In the past, we suspended and expelled difficult children from school. We now know that when we do this, the student usually becomes a dropout. Every effort must be made to keep students in school. If, however, a student's behavior represents a clear threat to the health and safety of others, we may have to educate her in isolation from other students. How this is handled varies according to each locale's resources.

ACADEMIC MANAGEMENT CONSIDERATIONS

Academic Enhancers

There are many things a teacher can do to make school more interesting, as follows:

1. Rewards, such as small edibles, stickers, or a good note.

2. Interest stimulators, such as making a movie or giving a play, having a mock funeral to bury "I can't," planting an Arbor Day tree, having an academic contest with a rival class, launching a balloon (balloons contain notes asking for the finder to write the class a letter).

3. Activity day is a great way to reward. Spring it on the class after a particularly on-task session. Well-chosen academic games can be included.

4. Demonstrations, experiments, guest speakers, and field trips pique interest.

5. Classroom newspaper published monthly, where articles are chosen and edited by the students, is a good project.

6. Involvement in real-life situations, such as attending a courtroom session.

7. Computers are a rapidly growing source of interest.

8. Take time to rewrite word problems using your students' names or situations they are familiar with.

9. Teacher enthusiasm is often the magic that turns a mundane lesson into an event.

10. Referral to the principal for commendation and the privilege of having a brown-bag lunch with a favorite teacher are powerful motivators.

11. Grades as rewards can be rewarding, particularly if you allow students to have a grade changed and raised by making corrections or by doing extra learning.

12. Recordkeeping can inspire students as they see IEP requirements being checked off as they are achieved. "Well, Mary, 5 down and 3 to go" is an encouraging kind of remark.

13. Positive recognition and praise are powerful motivators. "Wow!" "Look at you!" "You did it!" "Wait till your mom hears about this!"

Involving the Parents In Meaningful Ways

Despite the hustle and bustle of modern life, most parents do care about their children and want them to have a good education. Since parents can be enlisted to support your efforts in the classroom, you should be in regular contact with them.

Some teachers use the weekly contract as the vehicle to do this. Under this system, the parent is told (in person or by mail) that the student will bring home her work contract for the current week on Monday. As the student turns in various assignments, the teacher corrects them and initials the square when they are satisfactorily completed. By regularly consulting the contract, the parent has a record of how the student is doing.

Phone calls or personal contacts between teachers and parents once a month allow for that two-way exchange that is so valuable to having parents feel that you are interested in their child.

Parents who spend 15 minutes a night talking in detail to their child about what's happening at school or listening to their child read soon learn how much they enjoy this activity. Needless to say, there is usually a corresponding rise in the student's scores.

Many teachers like to use parents in the classroom to help students stay on-task. They can also help reinforce what the teacher is teaching. Parents are more likely to participate in this way if the following happens:

1. You give them a specific time and day that you will need their help.

2. You let them know what you want them to do.

3. You let them get the feel of working with individual students before giving them a group.

4. You and the students show appreciation for their services. (Applauding them or saying "Thanks" in unison is often enough.)

Involving the Principal in a Positive Way

Except in the most dire and rare circumstances, it is better to handle discipline problems yourself rather than to involve the principal. If it is an ongoing problem, you may want to tell him of your efforts so that if he becomes involved, he is aware of all the things you have already done to work with the situation.

Principals respond positively to being involved positively. If you're doing a successful activity in the classroom, the principal might be invited. Students like to show off. A trip to the principal's office can become a motivator. Let students who are doing fine work or showing good improvement take papers to show the principal. This is particularly effective with the troublesome child when she begins to do good work. Ask the principal to show approval and to give praise.

The Case for Cooperative Learning

Students today need to learn how to work with other people. The inability to work with others is frequently cited as a major cause of a person's termination from a job. Today, school is the best place to learn these skills because it is, for many youngsters, the only place where they interact with large numbers of people. In earlier days when large extended families were the rule and not the exception, these skills were learned at home.

Students need many opportunities to think aloud. Brainstorming is an important skill to teach. It is enriching for students to toss out their ideas and to receive feedback on them. It is equally important to teach students how to give feedback in a sensitive, constructive way.

Cooperative learning tenets include the following:

1. Students are placed in groups of four. A sociogram helps. Ask students to name three people they'd like to work with and three they would rather not work with. Try to see that they are in a group with at least one friend and no enemies.

2. A project is assigned. If it is to be a research paper, one paper is submitted for the group—not four individual papers.

3. Time is allotted for the students to plan and execute the project. The group decides on roles such as speaker, scribe, leader, mediator, or observer. Essential to the cooperative learning process is the understanding that each member is to contribute to the project, that one grade will be assigned, and that the grade may be skewed unfavorably if someone in the group has not participated fully.

   For example, if the project is to study the spelling list for a test, the group should understand that the scores of all four group members will be averaged to produce a single score given to all members of the group. Stronger group members therefore need to assume the responsibility to help weaker members to learn the spelling words so that the average score will be higher. Be careful, when assigning your students to groups, that the groups are heterogenous. If all the bright children are in one group, the dull ones in another, it will not generate the maximum learning. It is also important that girls and boys not be segregated into groups.

4. During the time the groups are working, the teacher and assistant should be circulating among the groups to check to see that they are functioning adequately in the following ways:

    a. That they are on-task
    b. That all members are getting an opportunity to talk or help
    c. That they get help from the teacher with the subject matter when they start to lag or to have other problems.

    Praise such as "Good point, John." "That's it, Sally. You helped John clarify his thinking" assists in skills development.

Cooperative learning lends itself to many subjects. If, for example, in math each student has 10 problems, all students in the group go over the problems and answers to see if they agree. When all 40 are done, they are submitted for a grade. On tests, individual scores may be tallied to yield a composite score for all members of the group. This encourages the members in the group to teach the laggards so that their scores do not adversely affect the others. Similar techniques can be used in English.

Social studies and science are also subjects for cooperative learning projects and experiments that can be done by the group.

Providing Adequate Learning Opportunities

Reading and math books sometimes do not provide enough exposure for students to learn a concept. It is often necessary to supplement them with additional practice pages.

Once a student understands a process, homework is an excellent way to provide additional drill. Remember: It is better to get back 5 to 10 problems done than to have a student refuse to do the assignment because it was too long.

Increasing Retention

Maximizing feedback.   As silly as it sounds, I feel compelled to say it anyway: The greater the amount of feedback and the higher degree of on-task behavior, the more likely it is that students are learning. Students need lots of opportunities to test, clarify, and refine their ideas. Students take in information and try to coordinate it with previously learned information. They must know whether or not it makes sense. I am reminded of a sixth grader who was fluently reading about climate. I asked, "What's climate, Tom?" His answer, "You take a mountain and climb it." Obviously our ideas were not the same. Hence, we need to develop ways to maximize feedback and clarification. Cooperative learning offers one way. The following are some other ways:

1. Ask a question. Have students work in pairs and come up with an answer.

2. Ask a question. Have students write the answer on a chalkboard or on a card that is held up and flashed to the teacher. (A joint journal is another possibility.)

3. Ask a question. Give students time to think about it, and on a given signal they should give the answer with a signal. Thumbs up means yes; thumbs down means no; thumbs sideways means, "I don't know." Answers can also be coded. For example, "I'm going to name an object. If you think it is a liquid, make an L with your fingers; if you think it is a solid, make a fist; if you think it is a gas, stick out your tongue."

Use of Higher-Level Questions, Imagery, and Visualization and Verbalization

Some questions involve merely repeating facts or paraphrasing. Others involve analyzing information and doing something new with it. Research shows that higher-level questions are more likely to help students retain information.

Lower level	"What was the Boston Tea Party?"
Higher level	"Compare the outcome of the Boston Tea Party then with how a similar incident of protest would be handled now. Write a modern-day news article titled, "Tea in the Sea."
Lower level	What is 4 + 8?
Higher level	Make up an addition story problem to go with the numbers 4 and 8. For grade 4 and up, tell the student, "Interview your mom or dad. Can they make up an addition, subtraction, multiplication, and division story problem for the numbers 4 and 8?" They should bring their story problems in writing to share with the class.
Lower level	Summarize the story you just read.
Higher level	What was the problem in this story? Have you ever been in a similar situation? Tell me about it. How was your situation the same or different? How did you resolve it? Do you think you'd resolve it differently now?
Lower level	Find all the key words in the story that describe the main character.
Higher level	Rewrite the story giving the main character a different personality and the story a different ending.

As we devise lessons, we use the lowest level of questioning when we use activities, such as:

1. Matching

2. Filling in blanks

3. Multiple choice

4. Defining

5. Summarizing (telling in your own words).

Initially these activities are all right, but we also need to move on to activities requiring application and analysis, such as:

1. Keep a diary that records both events and feelings.

2. Make a collection (involves classification).

3. Draw or make a map.

4. Illustrate a story.

5. Make a graph.

6. Classify.

7. Make a diorama.

8. Develop a survey.

9. Make up good test questions for what was studied. (Let students choose the best questions to use on a test.)

10. Write a report.

11. Compare and contrast.

12. Dissect.

13. Construct several questions to ask on an interview, and then interview some adult.

Finally, we want students to involve students in creating and evaluating, with activities such as the following:

1. Write a script for a play about . . . Get a friend to critique it.

2. Write an ad, draw a cartoon, write a story about . . .

3. Make a product.

4. Role-play an incident. Get the group to tell what it believes is going on; how the players feel.

5. Compose a song or poem.

6. Debate a question.

7. Write an editorial about . . .

8. Discuss (group activity).

9. Participate as a panel member.

10. Hold a mock court trial.

Imagery is another skill that can be taught. It can help students retain what they learn. When trying to memorize material to recall later, imagery can assist.

I once had a student who was taking a spelling test that contained *ie* words and *ei* words. He said he'd never pass it since he couldn't remember which way it went in a given word. Here is the list:

chief	*niece*
field	*brief*
believe	either
seize	ceiling
fierce	*pierce*
leisure	*piece*
vein	

We made up the following story, using imagery and all the *ie* words. "A fierce Indian chief ran across a field. My niece believes she will pierce his heart with a piece of sharp wood so he will die in a brief time."

He made a 100% because he knew that any word not included was spelled with an *ei*. Months later when he had occasion to spell *field* and *niece*, he still remembered the sentences involving the imagery.

Recently a colleague was teaching her students to count to 5 in Japanese using association:

1	e che
2	(ne)
3	san
4	she
5	go

Even the dullest students were able to immediately hold onto the information after seeing the teacher scratch her "itchy knee" (1, 2) drive her *Nissan* (2, 3), and *she go* (4, 5).

Use of visualization and verbalization is an essential skill to teach students so that they are able to comprehend what they have read. Students change words they read into mental pictures and tell you what they would put on the stage if they were directors of a movie or play. To illustrate: A sentence says, "Tom's horse reared and bucked when the lightning flashed."

Say to the student, "Get up and show me what the horse did." To stimulate the student to imagine more clearly, you might say, "If you were a movie director, what time of day would be best for making the lightning more scary—day or night?" Help the student to see that it would be more dramatic against a night sky.

Another sentence says, "The Indian boy had never been out to hunt before and he was scared." Ask the student, "How old is this boy? What kind of hair does he have? What is he wearing? Help me see him as you imagine him." Sometimes after the student describes "her" Indian, I'll describe "mine." If hers had on buckskins, I'll say that mine had on a loincloth. If hers had cropped hair, mine had a braid. If hers had on moccasins, mine will be barefoot. It is important to let the student know that your picture is not necessarily right and hers wrong and to help her to see how the author might want to be more detailed in a description.

Since children often lack words to explain concepts such as "cropped hair," they gesticulate. Much language development can occur as you give them the words they need. It is important to reinforce this by repeating their gesture and by saying, "What's hair like this called?" (A set of visualization and verbalization cards appears at the end of this chapter.)

Probing and Thinking Time

Many students have not learned to think. They have learned to wait, knowing that if they just say, "I don't know" long enough or if they shrug, the teacher or some other student will answer, letting them off the hook.

Sometimes I just say to a student, "Mary, I'm not going to tell you the answer. Here, I'll put the question up on the board. You can think about it and we can talk during recess." I then go on to the next question. I have found that by recess, the student will usually have an answer in mind.

Effective Lesson Design

There are at least three major aspects to the designing of an effective lesson, as follows:

1. Deciding what to teach.
2. Planning and delivering a lesson.
3. Evaluating your lesson with an eye toward improving the effectiveness of further lessons.

"*What shall I teach?*" In some districts, this has been decided for you. There are detailed courses of study for each grade, as well as for special education. Skills, naturally, fall in a sequential line. Some districts have courses of study that can be purchased for a nominal fee.

A variation of this pattern occurs where teachers choose what to teach learning-handicapped students from the offerings of a regular grade's course of study or books. Teachers of special day classes often end up using the regular education texts of a lower grade—for example, a fifth grade learning-handicapped student gets a third grade science book.

"*What shall I teach if there is no prescribed course of study?*" Some teachers would give their next month's salary to be in this position. They would see it as a way to be creative and to make learning fun. While writing units of study is a time-consuming project, it can be very rewarding.

If you find yourself in this position, look at it as a challenge. Diagnostic-prescriptive teaching can be highly effective since it involves finding and meeting the needs and interests of your particular students—to the end that the deficit area no longer exists. As a pretest, you may use standardized tests or teacher-made tests.

In language arts, social studies, and science or health, you can opt for one of the following:

1. Do a survey of student interests.
2. Select subjects you are enthusiastic about.
3. Select subjects you feel every educated person needs to know about.

Importance of Setting Goals

In sports, the goals are clear: to hit a home run, to throw a pass, to jump a hurdle. By setting goals, we will often exert our energies until we reach them. Likewise, we need to have high expectations for ourselves and for our students and to encourage them to set goals for themselves.

For the teacher, goal-setting means diagnostic-prescriptive teaching. First, we have to determine what it is that students need to learn and then to decide how we are going to get there.

Consider the case of two students. On a diagnostic reading placement test, they both score at beginning grade 2 level, but they had very different needs. For instance, John is a visual learner. He has learned to read by the sight-say method and can recognize only those words that he has memorized. He is confused by words that are very similar (for example, *though, thought, through*). He reads at a good pace but makes many careless errors because he does not demand sense from what he reads. Jane also reads at beginning second grade level, but she uses phonics to read. Her pace is slower, but she is accurate and her comprehension is excellent.

For John, the goals would be to build his awareness of phonetic elements and to teach him to demand sense from what he reads. For Jane, the goal would be to teach her to commit frequently used words to the automatic level so that her reading pace improves.

John would benefit from structural-analysis exercises and visualization and verbalization techniques, while Jane would benefit from flash cards, configuration exercises, and spelling exercises.

Both students can participate in the same reading group. You will want to vary their seatwork and your approach to them during the lesson. For example, when John confuses *saw* for *was*, you may say, "John, let me read that sentence the way you did," making the same error he did. Then you should ask, "Does that make sense? Look at this word" (point to *was*) and ask, "Does it begin with s[hiss] or w[make w sound]?" After he answers, ask him if he wants to change the way he read the sentence. Have him practice spelling the offending word. For seatwork, it would be beneficial for John to paraphrase what he read—first orally, then in writing.

For Jane, allow her to read a sentence or paragraph silently once or twice before she reads it aloud. For seatwork, Jane would probably benefit most from recreational reading at her easy-reading level.

In prescribing for students, you may have a broad goal that you wish to teach, but you may need to break down that goal into smaller tasks. For example, if your goal is to teach students to write paragraphs, think about the many learning skills necessary to do that.

Two prerequisite skills are the ability to spell and the ability to construct a proper sentence that makes sense. If these skills are missing, obviously the student cannot be taught to design a good paragraph.

Assuming that the student has the prerequisite skills, what should you teach her first? Second? Just for fun, you may wish to make a list of sequential tasks. I will then give you a suggested list for comparison, one that may not match yours at every point, but it will give you a good idea of the necessary skills.

Step 1. Teaching what a paragraph is. This involves more than parroting the definition, "A paragraph is a group of words or sentences relating to a given topic." It includes the following:

    a. Do the students recognize the format of a paragraph? You can determine this by handing them a page of print that involves several paragraphs and asking them to count the paragraphs and show you (signal the number) with their fingers. For those who miss, it is crucial that they understand that each time the author indents, there is a paragraph. (By counting the indentations, we can determine the number of paragraphs.) If this was not understood in the beginning, practice until the students can do that.

    b. Do the students understand that paragraphs vary in the number of sentences included? Help them to develop this understanding by counting sentences within sample paragraphs (by counting periods). Help them to develop a feel for what the reasonable sentence limit of a paragraph is by analyzing what authors actually do. Children in grade 2 can look at fourth grade texts and keep a tally. Here is an example:

p. 1	paragraph 1	3 sentences
	paragraph 2	5 sentences
	paragraph 3	1 sentence
	paragraph 4	6 sentences
	paragraph 5	8 sentences

    Help them to understand that if a paragraph gets too long (over 10 sentences), it may need to be broken into smaller units (small paragraphs).

    c. Do the students understand how to locate the main idea of a paragraph? Using sample paragraphs, ask the students to find the main idea and to underline it. This skill is extremely important, and it often takes weeks of practice to become skillful at doing it. While teaching this skill, the students should be repeatedly told that good writers usually put the main idea first or last. It will occur first more often than last, but it is a poor paragraph if the main idea falls within the paragraph.

    d. Do the students understand that all other sentences in the paragraph must relate to that main idea? This concept can best be developed by copying some paragraphs and then just throwing in a totally unrelated idea. The students are then asked to cross out the idea that does not belong or support the main idea. When students first begin this kind of practice, the errors need to be blatant ones. As students gain in their ability to analyze paragraphs, you can make the errors more subtle.

Remember that all of these tasks can be almost fun if made into a game as students keep score of how they did:

Day 1   3/6
Day 2   5/6
Day 3   6/6
Day 4   6/6   3 days = 100% = mastery
Day 5   6/6

Step 2.   Beginning to write simple paragraphs. This skill can be developed in a variety of ways, for example:

    a. Give the students a series of pictures. They write sentences to go with each picture and then rewrite the sentences using paragraph form. (Indent; put main idea first; add a summary sentence.)

The paragraph may look like this:

Fishing

Sam is going fishing. When he gets to the pond, he baits his hook. Suddenly, he gets a bite. He jerks his pole and out comes a fish.

b. Give the students a series of sentences. Then decide how to organize them. Limit the number of sentences to 3 to begin with. Increase the number as the students become more proficient. Here is a sample:

Like all insects, butterflies have six legs.
Butterflies also have antennae and wings.
Butterflies are insects.

becomes

Butterflies are insects. Like all insects, butterflies have six legs. Butterflies also have antennae and wings.

When the students get good at doing this skill, you may want to give them 8 or more sentences to organize into paragraphs (a mini-report), like the following:

Like all insects, butterflies have six legs.
Butterflies also have antennae and wings.
Butterflies are insects.
Butterflies begin as eggs.
The butterfly's life can be divided into four stages.
Eggs hatch into larva, which are sometimes called caterpillars.
The adult butterfly emerges from the cocoon.
Later the caterpillars spin cocoons around themselves.
While in the cocoon, the caterpillar changes into a butterfly.

becomes

Butterflies are insects. Like all insects, butterflies have six legs. Butterflies also have antennae and wings.

The butterfly's life can be divided into four stages. Butterflies begin as eggs. The eggs hatch into larva, which are sometimes called caterpillars. Later the caterpillars spin cocoons around themselves. While in the cocoon, the caterpillar changes into a butterfly.

Step 3. Advanced paragraph writing occurs when students demonstrate that they can create their own main idea and supportive details. Here the techniques of brainstorming and clustering (see Chapter 5) and outlining can be taught.

Step 4. Advanced analysis and evaluation of paragraph writing or editing are the highest paragraphing skills taught. Students critique their own work and the work of other students or other writers. They discuss ways to improve the authors' effectiveness by improving choice of words or wording, or by changing punctuation to reflect mood.

The task-analysis just described can be made into a unit of study that takes several months to teach. When you analyze a task, you should establish a time-line for its development.

What Steps Should a Good Lesson Include?

Research has shown that effective teachers seem to follow similar patterns of skill attack. They do the following:

1. Begin the lesson by gaining student attention.

2. State their goals or objectives so that students know how they will use the skills or information being taught.

3. Where appropriate, relate new learning to previous learning (short review of about 5 to 8 minutes).

4. Give input in small, sequential steps—clear, snappy, well-paced lessons of 11 to 15 minutes of input seem to stimulate student listening.

5. Use active guided practice, higher-level questions, and creative methods of increasing student response to check for student understanding of the lesson.

6. Give immediate feedback to students as to the correctness of the response.

7. Provide for continued practice under teacher supervision until students have mastered a skill.

8. Provide for periodic reinforcement of previously mastered skills.

Visualization and Verbalization Cards

The following sample paragraphs can be used in teaching visualization and verbalization skills:

At the circus, there were three rings. <u>In ring one</u>, a bear danced on top of a drum. <u>In ring two</u>, elephants paraded in a circle, trunk holding tail. <u>In ring three</u>, a lady made two lions jump from chair to chair through a ring of fire.

She had always wanted ice skates—white lace-up ones with silver blades.

These skates were ugly. Brown boots with black laces and blades that were scratched.

It was a tiled room. White square tiles on walls and floors. The floor slanted to the middle where there was a drain hole. On each side of the room were cages—dogs barked, cats meowed. The smell was awful.

Grandma and I like to walk in the woods. We came to a pond. In it are tiny tadpoles. All around the pond are weeds. A duck's nest is there with eggs in it.

Grandma let us bake cookies. We cut them into shapes—seven stars, six moons. We sprinkled sugar and cinnamon on the moons and put silver sprinkles on the stars.

He was a cute puppy—with floppy ears and a circle of black fur around one eye. He nibbled at my ankle and whimpered until I picked him up.

I opened the lunch box I found—a smushy pear fell out. The sandwich had turned green. Half-eaten cookies lay sadly stuck to the bottom. What a mess!

He had always wanted to be a clown. Tonight he was. He put a huge, curly wig on, painted his lips too big and too red. He painted on green eyebrows. His shoes were enormous floppy clown shoes. His costume was baggy with a ruffle at the neck.

Sitting in rows they waited. Some read. Some watched the clock. Some talked. A little girl pranced up and down the rows on tiptoe. A whistle blew. There was a loud roar and then a screech. Hooray! I'm on my way!

He sat by the campfire—stick in hand, roasting a marshmallow.

Oh, no. It was on fire. He blew out the flame. Too late. His marshmallow was black. Breaking off the black crust, he found the center to be wonderfully gooey and very good.

The children were playing in the snow. It was colorful. Red gloves, black snowboots, and yellow raincoats. Two snowmen appeared—one with an Abraham Lincoln hat. The other with black charcoal buttons all the way down its front.

Standing on a wooded cliff, Sandy saw a ribbon of a road winding through the valley below.

[Draw a picture to illustrate the words.]

Her face was flushed. Beads of sweat ran down the sides of her face. A drop fell from the end of her nose. She panted after her long, hot run. Had she won the race?

A siren sounded in the distance. Black smoke curled under the door. We crawled along the floor to the window, holding wet washrags over our noses and mouths to keep the smoke out.

Ida rowed her boat as fast as she could. Waves crashed against it, spraying her and leaving her soaked to the skin.

Finally she reached the drowning animal. Gathering all her strength, she lifted it into the boat. Four legs kicked wildly. It lay exhausted on the floor of the boat. She had saved its life.

The sun shone. The water glistened. Sea gulls floated on soft sea breezes. Waves licked the shore gently, leaving tiny sea crabs to the job of digging their way quickly into the sand, rather than becoming sea gull dinner.

Oh boy! There was something big on the end of Tom's pole.

He pulled and pulled until he landed his catch. What a disappointment!

It was a snowy day. The hill was covered. Sam didn't have a sled but he had a cardboard box. That would do.

Suzy picked a dandelion puff. She blew and blew until every little parachute was airborne. They floated to the ground. She threw the empty stem down and made a wish.

The horse trotted about the corral. They called him "Paint" because he looked as if someone had thrown paint on him. His swishing tail showed his happy mood.

Dr. Smith held the telephone between his head and shoulder. His hands clung to a very upset dog.

"What?"

"He'll either learn to climb down or fall out," he said.

He sat with his legs crossed—chin resting in his hands, thinking.

"I wish I hadn't done that. Now I'm in trouble. My dad will punish me."

Lights glared. Feet scuffled. Odd smells reached her nose. People wearing caps and masks passed—not speaking, not smiling. She felt like a plastic doll just lying there on that narrow white cart with a sheet pulled up to her chin. Would she be all right? Who knows? Who cares?

First Jim found several large round rocks that he arranged in a fire ring. Next he found many small sticks that he placed in the center of the ring. On top of the sticks he placed larger hunks of wood. He rolled up a paper, lit the end, and held it to the sticks.

Sally was so thrilled she cried and laughed at the same time. She held her Oscar in the air with one hand, and blew a kiss to the audience with the other.

Huge waves crashed on a small rocky island. In the night, the lighthouse signal flashed over and over and the horn blared its warning, "Watch out—watch out—watch out!"

The campfire had died down to red coals. Sam crawled into his sleeping bag. Lying there in the dark, he heard an owl and the noise of sticks breaking in the woods. He pulled his head into his bag and waited in fear. What was it?

Having nothing to do, we took a blanket outside and lay down on it. Watching the clouds, I said, "That one looks like a pear."

A basket on her head, held by one hand to steady it, she walked the dusty road to the village. A cow or ox had passed this way. She jogged to avoid the droppings. When she looked down the road, it seemed such a long way. Suddenly she was jarred. The contents of the basket lay beside her on the ground.

Multicolored stripes ran the length of the white sports car. The long-haired young driver slid from behind the wheel. Closing the door gently, the proud owner patted the hood and murmured, "Be good till I come back. I love you."

Teacher Self-Evaluation

Self-evaluation or self-critiquing leads to improved performance. The following form may prove helpful to you.

FORM FOR TEACHER SELF-EVALUATION

Room Environment

1. How does my room look? Will it be attractive to students? Would a parent be positively impressed?
2. Are bulletin boards and displays current? Functional?
3. Is the furniture appropriately arranged for the activity planned?
4. Is equipment or materials needed close at hand?
5. How is the temperature? How is the ventilation? How is the lighting?

Preplanning

1. Are my goals and objectives clear to me? Why do I want to teach this?
2. How will I get students settled quickly? Is there a short review activity they can do while I take care of the first 5 minutes of problems? If so, what?
3. What details must I take care of as they enter the room?
4. Does the aide have a clear idea of what is to be done? How can I ensure that we are working together?
5. What will I do to get students' attention?
6. How will I help students relate this lesson to previous lessons?
7. How can I help students see that they need to learn what is being taught? (Will they be tested on it? If so, how? Is it a career skill? Is it a life skill?)
8. How can I encourage student responsibility?
9. What input is necessary to teach this skill? Can it be taught in a single session? If not, how many sessions will I need? What shall I teach first?
10. What materials are needed for input? Audiovisual equipment or props? Charts? Diagrams?
11. How long will the input last? How can I enliven the input? Vary pace? Vary tone of voice? Vary loudness?
12. How will I check for understanding?
13. If some students don't catch on, what other approaches will I use?
14. Which students need to be given encouragement and positive self-esteem remarks?
15. What reinforcers do I need?
16. When will I be satisfied that they know the skill?
17. How many higher-level questions am I asking? (Write them down—it will ensure that you don't forget.)
18. What will faster students do when they finish an assignment?
19. Have I kept pencil and paper tasks meaningful? (Not busywork).
20. Have I planned a success-oriented lesson?
21. When and how will I give feedback—knowledge of results to the student?
22. How often do I need to reinforce this lesson to maintain the skill developed?

Post-Lesson Critique

1. To what extent was the lesson successful?
2. Who learned what?
3. Who and what needs more teaching?
4. What went well—why? What went poorly—why?
5. Were my directions clear?
6. Was the time spent passing papers or materials minimized?
7. Were the students attentive?

8. Was the pace lively?
9. Did student behavior reflect that schoolwork is a serious business?
10. How were successful students rewarded? Grade? Praise? Tangible reward?
11. Did positive remarks far outweigh negative remarks?
12. Did I dignify responses that were partially correct?
13. Did I avoid repeating the same thing ad nauseam?
14. How was my voice tone?
15. Did I feel in control?
16. What would I do differently?
17. How would a principal or parent have viewed the situation? Orderly? Quiet? Confused? Chaotic?
18. How did I relate to my students? Sarcastic? With humor?
19. Were critical thinking skills encouraged? Give examples.
20. Was there a high level of correct responses—80 + % or better? Were all students participants? If not, whom do I need to be concerned with? How can I involve them next time?
21. Are there ways I could have increased the on-task behavior?
22. If students interacted, was the quality of their interaction positive? Did they compliment and encourage each other?
23. If any situation occurred where the lesson was interrupted by discipline, how could I have precluded this from happening? Did I handle it swiftly? Fairly? Without showing partiality? Firmly but with concern for the child's dignity?
24. What did the aide think of the lesson? Was he actively involved? Does he feel satisfied with what he is doing? Would he like to participate more fully in the classroom? How?
25. If students are older, what did they think? What suggestions do they have for my improvement?
26. In what ways did I allow students to share ownership in the classroom—who was a monitor (passing or collecting papers, giving help, running errands)?

4

INTERVENTION WITH LEARNING-DISABLED STUDENTS

Teaching learning-disabled students is fascinating work. Analyzing and providing for each student's unique needs is challenging and rewarding. This chapter and the next should be viewed as a menu from which you can select ideas that seem applicable to a particular student's needs.

TECHNIQUES FOR ELIMINATING FAILURE SYNDROME AND BUILDING SELF-ESTEEM

Each person has a mental balance sheet on which are recorded pluses and minuses from our experiences. When the pluses exceed the minuses, the person feels positive about himself. When we believe that we have failed more often than we have succeeded, we are defeated—we experience failure syndrome and may indeed become mentally ill unless the deterioration is stopped and reversed.

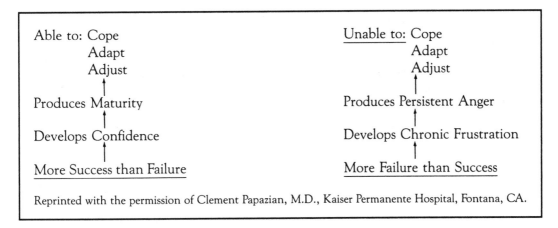

Reprinted with the permission of Clement Papazian, M.D., Kaiser Permanente Hospital, Fontana, CA.

Problem: Federal regulations governing eligibility for special education services require that a child be significantly behind before receiving help. Therefore, many children entering our classes are well into failure syndrome and have already suffered loss of self-esteem.

Solution: One of the first tasks facing us is to replace the "I can't" attitude with a willingness to try. During the first week you are with students, you will want to talk about their feelings. (See Chapter 6, "Teaching Strategies for Success")

The following illustrates the importance of opening up and discussing feelings: Recently a sixth grade boy was very hostile, blurting out, "You think I'm dumb." In talking about the matter, he said that he had decided in kindergarten that he was dumb because the other children could read and he couldn't. He was still reading below grade level. We talked about the cause of his learning problem—chronic ear infections from 18 months to 3 years and the resultant slow acquisition of language. I told him of Thomas Edison's and Albert Einstein's school problems and of their life achievements. He was relieved. We made up a line he could use in regular class when children called him dumb. "No, I'm not dumb. I am behind because of a hearing problem I had as a kid." We practiced it daily until he could say it comfortably. Whenever he lapsed into his hostility, I'd say, "Now, Thomas Edison, you can do this," and he'd smile and be inspired to try it.

To break the failure syndrome, you can try the following:

1. Give short assignments that you are sure the student can do.

2. Give immediate feedback. As the student completes an answer, say, "Great," "Exactly right," "Wow!" If he misses, point to the error and very quietly say, "Look at this one again."

3. Give encouragement. Keep asking for just one more answer but watch for signs of weariness. When weariness sets in, compliment the child. "You're doing more and better every day. Thanks. Let's stop."

4. Avoid overkill. Whenever you can, divide long assignments into shorter ones. Once I handed a student 50 words she was to decode. She took a quick look at the list and said, "I can't do that!" I was taken by surprise because I knew that she could. She had been doing daily lists of 20 words of the same difficulty for weeks. I put the words on 2″ × 3″ cards—one word per card. She went right through them— 96% perfect. I then gave her the cards and the original list, and when she realized that they were the same, she said, "I didn't think I could do that. It looked like so much." She felt really proud of herself.

5. For daily practice work, do not put a grade on the paper until all the errors are corrected. Then you will be able to write, "Corrected to 100%." When students demonstrate that they have the skill, I give the test. Sometimes I don't tell them until they're finished that it was a test. Then I say, "That's great! You just got a 100% on that test!" Not knowing that it was a test prevents test-phobia, and if the student doesn't do well, you have the option of just allowing it to be corrected for a daily grade.

6. With learning-handicapped students, it is really important that in their daily work you give them experiences in the same format as will be used on the test. When presented differently, they often do not recognize the skill.

Early on, you will want to establish a close working relationship with the parents, one that provides for regular two-way communication. You will need to sell yourself. Oddly enough, your success with the student depends on your success in building a close, trusting relationship with the parents. Parents can help enormously at home by encouraging and supervising. If a child senses that the teacher and the parents are in agreement, he is less likely to balk.

Once in a long while, you will get a stubborn child who says, "I won't do this" (the power abuser). The child's school career is essentially over if you accept this. If you decide to challenge it, here are two tips.

First, discuss the matter with the parents. Generally they are getting the same treatment at home. If they are willing, set up a time to work with the child after school when there is no audience.

Second, be certain that the assignment is something that he can do, such as unscrambling spelling words, a word search, or an open-book quiz. It should be a very short assignment.

Here is the story of one child. She was a fourth grader. She threw temper tantrums—cried, stomped, hit things (not people). One day her mother came to get her just as school was over. I said that she had not done her work yet—5 subtraction problems and asked if I could keep her and take her home when it was done and corrected. The mother said yes. I said, "Don't worry about us. I'll have her home by nine o'clock at the latest." I walked the mother out to the end of the hall. When I returned in less than 3 minutes, the child had the problems done correctly. Years later in talking with her (she still visits), she said that she had always been able to intimidate her teachers. That day when she could see that I meant to call her bluff, she had weighed whether it was worth it to be stubborn and miss dinner and 4 hours of TV or to do the 5 problems. She said that she had wanted limits but that no one had ever set them. Miraculously, with this child, this one time constituted a cure. Kindness, rewards, and encouragement are more likely to work than the tough approach, but none of these had worked on this child. Fortunately, she responded.

Failure syndrome in older students often comes in the form of absenteeism and truancy.

Your first task is to do all that you can to get the student to school. This may involve class changes to put him with the most effective teachers, and it may involve some payoff for attendance, such as free tickets to a game. It will almost always involve talking with him and finding ways to make the curriculum more relevant for him.

Many high schools have opted to offer an independent study program for students who find daily class attendance abhorrent. This is admirable, but great care needs to be given to set high standards for these programs.

In these programs, the student sees his teacher one-to-one for one or more times a week to obtain new assignments, to receive instruction, and to get feedback from previous assignments.

Building Self-Esteem

Self-esteem comes from the following feelings:

1. Worthiness
2. Belonging

3. Competence

4. Having some influence or power

It is to be recognized that children's feelings of esteem are highly influenced by their relationship with their parents. One of our jobs at school should be to help students do whatever they have to do for parental approval. Sometimes parents need help in seeing that their child is trying to please them and is making progress.

When parents are overburdened or worried, they are sometimes oblivious to the child's needs. For example, when marriages break down, the child usually loses self-esteem unless some intervention occurs. His sense of belonging is undermined; he feels insecure. He may feel alienated and guilty (fearing that he somehow has caused the problem). During this difficult time, the child's work will suffer. What can a teacher do to help?

It is appropriate to talk with parents during this time—to help them become aware of their child's fears about the future and possible guilt feelings. It is also appropriate to suggest that the child may need the help of a counselor to get through this difficult period. If the parents are in a custody battle or are having friction regarding visitation arrangements, it is imperative that you let them know that their battles are having an adverse effect on the child and on his schoolwork. Teacher warmth, concern, and understanding during this time are critical to both the child and the parents.

During this time, the child cannot take criticism. Feedback and work correction must be done gently. If possible, it is probably best to do it one-to-one before or after school or at lunchtime. This will allow you to listen if the child wants to share his concerns.

The illness or death of a parent can also produce the same feelings of guilt, loss, and alienation. Children often need professional help to get through these situations.

All children need to belong. These feelings of belonging are fostered when teachers (1) talk personally to the children, (2) use advance organizers [one of the cruelest things we do in school is allowing captains to choose teams because the children chosen last feel unappreciated], (3) send positive messages [see Chapter 3 on finding better ways to talk to children], (4) help students talk more positively to themselves [replacing the "I'm dumb" with, "I'm okay. I have strengths. I can accept or work around my weaknesses."], and (5) use cooperative learning.

Teachers can do much to increase the student's feelings of competence. As we give him skills (for example, by checking off IEP requirements), he sees that he's progressing. We want to replace "I can't" with "I can succeed." We want to teach the child to look first to himself for what *he* can do. If he needs additional help, we should teach him to consult friends, parents, or an authority.

I can remember my seventh grade teacher saying, "Educated people do not have to know everything, but they do have to know where to go to get help." Self-reliance should be encouraged.

Teachers can also do much to increase the student's self-esteem by increasing his feelings of control. When we teach a child that he cannot always control what happens to him but that he can always control his reaction to a situation, we help him learn to cope.

If a person believes that he has no control over his situation, that he is a victim, his self-esteem is nil. We have to teach children that they always have control—even in desperate situations. For example, if a person gets cancer and is told he will die, he can lie down and die, or he can say, "I'll change my diet. I'll change my life-style. I'll get busy doing something about this." There are many documented cases of remission that have followed such changes of attitude.

The child can go to pieces over his parents' divorce or he can confront his fears and talk to them about what is worrying him. He can get busy with his own interests and distract himself so that worry does not consume him.

As teachers, we have to confront students who are making excuses. For example, if the child says, "I didn't do my homework because I forgot it," we need to say that that is not acceptable. We have to help them see that an employer will not accept "I forgot" as an excuse. Teaching this lesson is easy for me. My students have seen me write notes to myself on the inner part of my wrist. They ask why, and I explain that I have a terrible memory, and I do it so that I don't forget. I make a point not to wash the message off until it's taken care of. Often I will suggest that they use the same technique to remember their homework. Sometimes they'll ask me to "tattoo" their wrist with a note such as "spelling HW."

Likewise, teachers must teach students that blaming others or blaming circumstances is not acceptable. "I forgot to do my homework because my mom made me go . . ." When students use this excuse, talk with them about how to handle this in the future. One way to handle this is to give students more than one night to get an assignment done. Caution them at the time that the assignment is given that excuses will not be accepted. Tell them not to procrastinate and to return the assignment early if it's done before the due date. Remind them of the upcoming assignment on intervening days.

LD students often talk to themselves in self-defeating ways. Their inner language is filled with, "Boy I'm dumb," "I'm clumsy," "I'm ugly," and so on. We can help them raise their self-esteem by having them practice saying, "I'm okay. I can learn to do this." Just as patriotism is taught with certain songs or the Pledge of Allegiance, if we have students say positive things to themselves often enough, they will believe them in time.

There is a very fine book that presents lots of practical ideas for fostering self-esteem. It is *100 Ways to Enhance Self-Esteem in a Classroom—A Handbook for Teachers and Parents* by Jack Canfield and Harold Wells (Prentice Hall, 1976).

In addition, the educational consulting team of Crane-Reynolds, Inc., has designed a very fine program for helping students from elementary through high school who need help in the social skills area. (See the list of sources of help at the end of this handbook for further information.)

Some interesting work is currently being done regarding personality and temperament. An effort is being made to relate this information to teacher and student temperament and to interpersonal interactions. If you wish to know more about this, read *Please Understand Me* by David Keirsey and Marilyn Bates (copyright Gnosology Books, Ltd.) Distributed by Prometheus Nemesis Book Co., P.O. Box 2748, 1984, Del Mar, CA, 92014.

TECHNIQUES FOR VISUAL PERCEPTUAL DEFICITS
AND VISUAL MOTOR DEFICITS

Visual perception is a process involving the receipt and interpretation of visual stimuli.

Problem: Some students may show a lack of attention to visual detail. For example, in younger students this may be a lack of understanding of the terms *alike* and *different* or it may be a lack of attention to detail.

*Find the one that is the same**

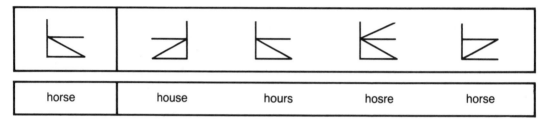

| horse | house | hours | hosre | horse |

*Find the one that is different.**

Solution: To remediate these kinds of deficits, provide the student with a variety of comparison experiences that involve the careful distinction of size, shape, color, and direction. At the beginning, the student will need some guidance. In the example just given, you may have to ask, "Are the houses the same size or is one bigger?" Point to the third one and say, "This one is a little bigger." Other comparison questions might be:

Do they all have a chimney?

Do they all have 2 windows?

Are the doors all the same shape?

Help the student verbalize his answer: "The third one is different because it is slightly bigger and has an arched doorway."

Also helpful are art experiences where the student is verbally directed to look for detail. For example, he draws the outline of his own hand, filling in lines for knuckles and fingernails. On an apple, he is directed to note that it is not uniformly red but shows dots or streaks of color.

Nature experiences are wonderful. I had a fourth grader this year who had never noticed that pine trees have needles, not leaves. He discovered this when we went for a walk and came back with a variety of leaves.

---

*These kinds of materials are commercially available.

Jigsaw puzzles can teach a lot about size, shape, and color. Begin with easy puzzles with fewer pieces (twenty-five for kindergarteners) and distinct color variations. Teach the student to make the border first and then to work inward by color. The quality of the student's work usually improves as his attention to and awareness of detail improve.

Problem: Many learning-disabled students report that they can see better when the amount of light on the work surface is diminished. This is particularly true when classrooms have fluorescent lighting.

Solution: Students who find this true can be assisted if you do the following:

1.   Have a variety of transparent plastic overlays available (smoked, green, yellow, blue) and allow students to choose the color that works best for them when they cover their work with it.

2.   Use photocopies instead of dittos. (Use blue paper instead of white paper.)

3.   Allow students to wear a visor in class if the overhead lighting bothers them.

4.   Allow students to wear lightly tinted sunglasses in class if they help.

Problem: Many students have difficulty copying accurately.

Solution: Whenever students are asked to copy material, they should be given some guidelines. "The purpose of this lesson is to copy accurately. Concentrate on getting every letter and every word right." "The purpose of this lesson is to improve your penmanship. Be sure to leave a space between each word and to form your letters carefully."

If students are copying from the chalkboard, assist them by keeping passages short, making sure that they have read them orally several times prior to copying, and by keeping the passage uncluttered, leaving large spaces between lines. Allow students to use a caret (∧) to insert any omitted words. Rarely can they recopy without making at least the same number of errors, and often their performance declines.

Students may be helped to copy by simply improving the way they sit to copy. They have to place materials correctly and follow with a finger on the nonwriting hand.

The index finger of left
hand holds place or a
marker can be held in place.

Writing hand

(Reverse the
placement of
book and paper
for left-handed
students.)

When attention and memory improve, students can copy more accurately.

Problem: Some students make reversals or inversions. Many learning-disabled students reverse letters and numbers (for example, *b/d*) or show inversion of letters (for example, *n/u*).

Solution: To remediate this problem, you need to focus the child's attention on the letters and numbers that are troublesome for him. This can be done in the following ways:

1. Tape a number line or letter strip on his desk or in his folder and insist that he refer to it. (A payoff for correct performance will often motivate him.)

2. Have the student practice one of the offenders daily. Write a model of the letter on the chalkboard in foot-high letters, pointing out where the letter or number should begin. The student then traces over the letter 25 times while you coach him to "feel where it begins," "feel which way it goes," "feel how it flows." When the student is proficient with one offender, add a second.

3. For *b/d* confusion, have the student turn his hands this way:

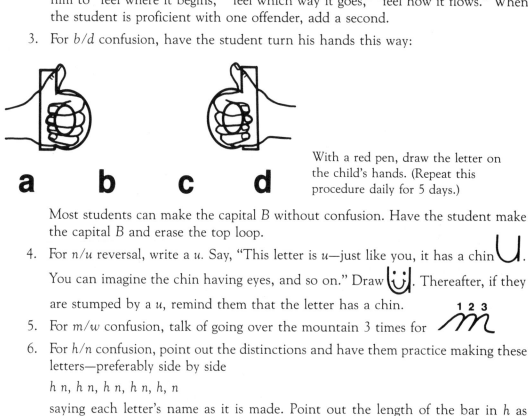

    With a red pen, draw the letter on the child's hands. (Repeat this procedure daily for 5 days.)

    Most students can make the capital *B* without confusion. Have the student make the capital *B* and erase the top loop.

4. For *n/u* reversal, write a *u*. Say, "This letter is *u*—just like you, it has a chin ⋃. You can imagine the chin having eyes, and so on." Draw ⎵·‿·⎵. Thereafter, if they are stumped by a *u*, remind them that the letter has a chin.

5. For *m/w* confusion, talk of going over the mountain 3 times for ⁱ²³ 𝓂

6. For *h/n* confusion, point out the distinctions and have them practice making these letters—preferably side by side

    h n, h n, h n, h n, h, n

    saying each letter's name as it is made. Point out the length of the bar in *h* as compared to *n*.

Similarly, for *n/r* confusion point out that the *r* stops in midair and is not brought to the base line.

Problem: Many students make sequencing errors. Another fairly common learning disability is the sequencing deficit: words that are similar in spelling are often confused. Common offenders include the following:

saw/was

on/no

there/three

being/begin/bring

through/though/thought

Solution: There are two ways to remediate this problem, as follows:

1. Teach the student to demand sense from what he reads. If the sentence he read didn't make sense, he needs to work on it again until it does.

2. Drill students specifically on these common offenders:

was/saw	They must check out the first sound to distinguish between them.
on/no	
There/three	They must look to see if the word has *here* in it (as in *here* and *there*) compared to the 2 *ee*'s on the end.

   th = r   *ee*

   (sound)

   b e (i n g) / b e g (i n) / b (r) i n g
   t h (r) o u g h / t h o (u g h) / t h o u g h (t)

Problem: Some students have visual figure-ground deficits. A figure-ground deficit occurs when one is not able to focus one's attention on a given stimulus while other visual stimuli are also present. Common difficulties include the following:

1. Losing one's place. Solution: Use a marker or finger when reading.

2. Not being able to work because of a movement in the room. Solution: Prohibit movement, or place students in a position where they won't see movement—for example, a corner facing a wall or a study carrel.

3. Not being able to copy accurately. Solution: Eliminate copying tasks or use techniques described earlier in this chapter.

4. Failing to see the central theme or picture. Solution: Discuss with students that illustrators put the central theme in the foreground and that it is the most prominent part of the picture and that while tiny details add interest, they are to look for the bigger picture.

5. Having a disorganized or cluttered work space. Solution: Help students clear their desks; have a place to keep all their belongings.

Problem: Often students have visual closure and visual association deficits. When presented with a word where the major portion of the word is there, some students cannot supply the missing letter. For example:

> h_lp (cannot supply the *e*), fr_end (cannot supply the *i*)

Solution:

1. Teach students to write the word by color-coding the missing *e* in red.

2. Teach students to systematically mispronounce words with offending letters. For example, if the word is *friend*—during practice sessions, they should call it "fry-end" so that they can hear the silent *i*.

3. Teach students to orally say letters and to use their bodies during practice sessions. For example, if the vowel is an *a*, they should tap their heads as they say the *a*. For *e*, their finger should be placed between their teeth; for *i*, they should touch the eye; for *o*, they should make an exaggerated *o*-motion with a hand, and for *u*, they should point skyward (up). This kinetic method seems to strengthen memory.

When given fill-in-the-blank dittos, many learning-disabled students cannot figure out what goes in the blanks. To solve this, teach students to read the sentence aloud all the way to the end, and to say, "bloomp" as they hit the blank and then to continue onward.

> The king had a _____ on his head.

> becomes

> "The king had a bloomp on his head."

Generally they will have no difficulty supplying the word *crown* because it makes sense. Marianne Frostig's *Program for the Development of Visual Perception* (Follett Publishing Co., 1973) is a kit of reproducible dittos. If you do not have this material, it is an invaluable resource for remediating the kinds of deficits just described.

Problem: Some students have visual perceptual deficits due to problems of visual muscular control. Many learning-disabled adults report the following:

1. The material appears out of focus.

2. The print swims around on the page.

3. The print is not uniformly black.

There has been much excitement over Ronald Reagan's declaration in his State of the Union Message that "we who are in government must take the lead in restoring the economy." The Democrats staged an explosion of applause in response to it, and both that moment and the sentence that gave rise to it have now been analyzed to death. Did it or didn't it mean that the president's critics had been vindicated, that Reagan newly accepts a central role for government in bringing the economy to heel, that he has—in his critics' terms —finally seen the light?

If you try to read this sample, you will have a greater appreciation for how difficult reading would be for those who experience this phenomenon.

Comprehension of the passage's content would probably be lost in the laborious task of struggling with the instability of the print. If, in addition, the person has faulty eye movements (skips lines, rereads lines), comprehension is further diminished. Persons with this problem often yawn or rub their eyes or complain that their eyes hurt, itch, or tear. They may also turn their paper or head to odd angles when reading.

To determine whether a student's eyes are tracking correctly, ask the student to follow the end of your pencil.

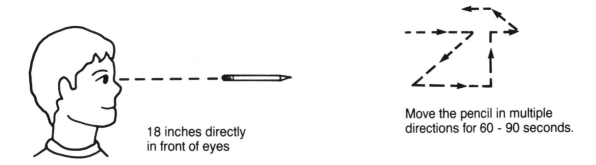

18 inches directly
in front of eyes

Move the pencil in multiple
directions for 60 - 90 seconds.

The two eyes should (1) move in unison, (2) move smoothly, and (3) be able to sustain the activity for 90 seconds.

To determine whether or not the student has a convergence problem, have the student focus on your pencil at 24 inches from his nose and tell him to continue to focus on it as you bring it right down to his nose. The eyes should cross (contrary to the old wives' tale, the eyes won't freeze that way). Now move the pencil back out as he follows it back to 24 inches away from his face. The student's eyes should perform this motion without jerkiness or loss of focus.

Solution: If you note problems of tracking or convergence, the student would probably benefit from some developmental visual therapy that may be available. If it isn't, we want to show understanding by doing the following:

1. Encourage the pupil to read with a finger or marker.
2. Shorten his reading assignments.
3. Teach him how to find and mark the most important passages—highlight the main ideas in pink, the supporting details in yellow.
4. Have someone read to him.
5. Allow him to read with one eye at a time.
6. Allow him to rest his eyes frequently.
7. Put some of the material on tape so that he can listen to it.

Problem: Some students have messy papers with too many erasures.

Solution: Give the student a pencil without an eraser. Instruct him to put a simple line through an error rather than obliterating the mistake. When you look at the paper, you will be able to see the original word and to judge whether the student is being too demanding on himself. Many LD students expect more of themselves than is necessary.

Problem: Many students have difficulty in cutting or pasting.

Solution: Students need to learn to do gross cutting first. Teach them to trim off and eliminate excess paper before doing finished cutting on the lines. When they are doing finished cutting, they should be taught to turn the paper as they go rather than to hold the scissors at odd angles. (Left-handed students should have access to left-handed scissors.)

In pasting, the amount and placement of the glue must be taught. Limiting the amount of glue available helps tremendously.

Problem: Some students have difficulty throwing and catching a ball, or jumping rope.

Solution: In throwing and catching a ball, the trick in catching it is to keep one's eye on the ball. The trick to throwing it is to keep one's eye on the ball's final destination. Give the child this information just before his turn. Jumping rope is a matter of rhythm rather than of watching the rope.

TECHNIQUES FOR REMEDIATING AUDITORY
PERCEPTUAL DEFICITS

Auditory perception is the process of receiving auditory stimuli and interpreting them on the basis of past experiences. The most valuable book I know of in remediating auditory deficits was developed by Selma E. Herr. It is titled *Teacher's Handbook for Developing Auditory Awareness and Insight*. It is a fine, comprehensive program complete with student response booklets. Program 1 covers preschool; kindergarten; and first, second, and third grades; Program 2 is for grades 4, 5, and 6; and Program 3 is designed for junior and senior high school students and adults. It is available through IMed Publishers, 11823 E Slauson Ave 40, Santa Fe Springs, CA 90670. I urge you to acquire a set appropriate to your students' needs. A second book that gives good information is Jerome Rosner's *Helping Children Overcome Learning Difficulties*, (Walker, 1975).

Problem: Some students have auditory processing deficits. Persons who have an auditory processing deficit cannot process what is said to them if it is delivered at a regular speaking speed. When a person habitually says "huh" or "what," we must suspect that he has this common problem. These persons do not benefit from lectures. They need to be shown.

Solution:

1. Repeat the information several times, or tape-record it so that the student can listen as many times as he needs to.
2. Speak more slowly, with frequent pauses (every 3 to 4 words).
3. Present the same information visually (directions, diagrams, notes on the chalkboard).
4. Assign a buddy who will go over the material again.
5. Teach the student to listen for and visualize the nouns and verbs.

Problem: Some students have auditory discrimination deficits. These persons are not able to discriminate between sounds. Common culprits include the plosive sounds *p*, *b*, *t*, *d*, *g*, *c*; the letter *l*; the vowel sounds *e* and *i*; and the final consonants *m* and *n*.

Solution: Students should be taken to a mirror to be shown and to practice various sounds. For example, they have to learn how the mouth should look for the vowels. They need to see that for the short *a*, the mouth is open wide enough "to bite an apple," but for an *e*, it is only partially open (about one finger's width), and for an *i*, it is almost closed. They need to feel how much air is necessary to produce a *p* or *t* as opposed to the *b* or *d*. They need for you to hold their hand next to your mouth as you produce these sounds. You must show them how to place the tongue for the *l* sound; where to place the teeth and lips for *m*, *v*, *f*, and how much air is needed for each sound. They need to see the difference between the *sh* and *s*. In the *s*, the air passes behind the front teeth. In the *sh*, the teeth are shut and the air escapes differently from the s. They need to feel how the air backs up in the nasal cavity for an n and in the throat for a g.

You may be saying, "I'd send the child to the speech therapist." While speech therapy is great, its efficacy is markedly increased when the teacher and parent both insist on the correct production of sound.

Students with auditory discrimination problems need to be encouraged to watch the lips of the speaker and to demand sense from what they hear.

Problem: Some students have auditory figure-ground deficits. People with this deficit usually have normal or acute hearing, but they cannot attend to the primary sound stimulus due to conflicting noises.

Solution:

1. A quiet classroom where one person speaks at a time

2. Notes on the chalkboard to emphasize major ideas

TECHNIQUES FOR ELIMINATING PERSEVERATION

Problem: For reasons that are not clear to us at this time, some LD individuals perseverate. Perseveration takes many forms. The following are some examples:

The person laughs longer and louder than others or claps longer.

When the person is asked to make 6 dots, 4 circles, or whatever, he makes many more than the required number.

The student gives the wrong answer over and over. He may even say, "No, that's not right" and then repeat the same answer again.

Solution: A hand on the shoulder or a "Stop" often helps. After a pause, you may be able to repeat the activity without having the perseveration reoccur.

TECHNIQUES FOR REMEDIATING DEFICITS IN SPATIAL AWARENESS AND BODY AWARENESS

A significant percentage of children who experience learning problems will also be deficient in their movement skills. Some will be described as clumsy, others as accident prone.

Problem: Some students have poor coordination of the large muscles.

Solution: In the United States, we once believed that through normal play our children would get the exercise they needed. Now, however, we realize that we need more supervised exercise designed to strengthen various body systems, such as the cardiovascular system and the arms. As some countries do, we need to insist on daily calisthenics. In the past, we taught students to be competitive, but now we have to modify that emphasis by stressing cooperation and teamwork and by encouraging each child to outdo his own previous performance.

In my opinion, a minimal program would be 30 minutes a day, and you would need the following:

1. A balance beam
2. Balls of varying sizes—tennis, baseball, dodgeball, basketball and hoop
3. At least 6 or 8 old tires
4. A scooter board
5. Jump ropes
6. Mats or a carpeted area
7. A Hula Hoop
8. Beanbags
9. A bat, a racket
10. Climbing bars, hanging bars
11. Small barbells (5 pounds)

Balance beam activities include walking forward and backward on the beam and are best done without shoes, with one's eyes straight ahead. An unsteady child may at first need to hold hands with someone walking beside the beam until he feels more certain. Later, the complexity of this skill can be increased by having the child walk with a beanbag on his head, or walk while bouncing a ball beside the beam, or walk and step over a beanbag placed every 15 inches to 18 inches, or by edging up the beam while turned sideways.

Ball activities would include batting practice by keeping one's eyes on the ball; catching and throwing activities; or tossing the ball at various targets.

The tires lend themselves to various activities such as the following:

1. Jumping rabbit fashion

Begin here
flat-footed.

2. Hopping on alternate feet

3. Tossing activities—tossing beanbags into the well of the tire.

The scooter board (a body board on roller skate wheels) would be used primarily for propelling oneself by the use of the arm muscles.

Likewise, bars for climbing and pulling up are needed. Today's toys are more likely to develop the leg muscles, but we need ones for the upper body and arms as well.

In the classroom, by means of art and health lessons, we need to help children improve their body knowledge. For example:

Week 1.   Draw an outline of a body on butcher paper.

Week 2.   Put in bones, pointing out how many are in the head.

Week 3.   Add spine, back, arm, leg, hands, feet.

Week 4.   Talk about how muscles attach to bones by ligaments (study ligaments in a chicken).

Week 5.   Draw an outline of a body again.

Week 6.   Show the location of the digestive system—mouth, esophagus, stomach, duodenum intestine. Discuss the digestive process.

Week 7.   Show the respiratory system—nose, mouth, esophagus, bronchial tubes, lungs. Discuss respiratory process.

Week 8.   Add the heart and talk about blood circulation.

Week 9.   Discuss the nervous system.

Week 10. Teach relaxation techniques.

Problem: Some learning-disabled students get lost or confused when they move about the school or their community.

Solution:

1. One of the earliest class activities should be daily walks (first week of school) around the campus. While walking, ask questions to direct their attention to details. For example, "How are the rooms numbered?" "What landmarks did we pass on the way to the library? restrooms? playground? cafeteria?"

2. Teach map skills to encourage awareness of environmental detail—for example, early in the year, have students work in groups of two to develop a school map.

You need to begin the map by showing the basic structure (first, outline the shape of the school and then note one area, such as the office or your classroom).

3. Teach directions N-S-E-W and relate these first to the school maps they have drawn and then to their community. (Teach them that the sun sets in the west and comes up in the east.)

4. Teach students to read local maps and to describe directions. Ask a question such as "How do I get from here to [name a common landmark]?" They must tell both the direction and the street: "You drive west on Fifth Street."

Problem: Students who are constantly getting hurt need special attention. They can be trained to be more aware of their surroundings. Clumsiness is often simply not paying attention to what one is doing.

Solution: Set up obstacle courses to be walked through. Talk them through activities: "Where is your finger? Where are the scissors? Go slower. Look at what you're doing."

TECHNIQUES FOR REMOVING CONCEPTUAL DEFICITS

Problem: In my experience, the most frequent causes of conceptual deficits are (1) a lack of language development and (2) a lack of experience.

Solution:

1. Provide guided experience in language and conceptual development through classroom lessons, audiovisual experiences, and field trips. Student feedback is an essential element.

2. Use visualization and verbalization activities to check student understanding.

3. Be alert to student need for information.

The following sample lesson is illustrative of solution 1. The objective of the lesson is to teach the concept of the word *container*.

Sample Lesson

Anticipatory set: Enter room; place a cup, box, and purse in a prominent place. Write on the chalkboard: "How are a cup, box, and purse the same?"

Input: Ask them to discuss your ideas in a group or with a friend. After a minute or two, let them contribute their ideas orally. They usually say, "You can put things in them." You have to tell them, "They are containers. All containers can hold something. The cup holds liquids [pour some out], the box holds objects [open and show], the purse holds objects."

Check for understanding: "I'm going to hold up an object. You are to decide if it is a container. Is it usually used to hold something? I'm going to give you time to think. When I say 1, 2, 3, answer, you may say *container*. If it is not a container, remain quiet.

> Display jar—allow 5 seconds think time—give signal for answer. After the group answer, confirm, "Yes, it is a jar; sometimes it holds mayonnaise [or whatever]."
>
> Display paper sack—think time—answer—confirm.
>
> Display pencil—think time—answer. You may get an argument here. Someone will say that it holds lead. Redirect: "Is its primary purpose to hold lead?" A discussion will allow students to clarify their ideas.

Guided practice: Working in your group, make a list of as many containers as you can in 10 minutes. (As they work, you and your aide should circulate, helping them clarify their ideas: "Does it hold something? What?")

At the end of 10 minutes, list all the answers (do not allow repeats) on chart paper (save the chart paper for future reference).

Independent practice: (This can be done orally or as homework on a ditto)

Item	*Container?*	*What does it hold?*
suitcase	_____	_____
hose	_____	_____
drawer	_____	_____
TV	_____	_____
refrigerator	_____	_____
window frame	_____	_____
bookcase	_____	_____
car	_____	_____
bike	_____	_____
baby crib	_____	_____

Next day: Discuss answers, reasoning. For a second day's homework, have them make a list of 2 containers not previously listed (they'll need the list from the chart). Enlist their parents'/sisters'/brothers' input.

The following example shows how I was able to work with one individual's conceptual needs.

In his reading book, a fifth grade student came to a sentence ". . . stood amid his friends." When he was asked to visualize what *amid* meant, it had no meaning at all to him. Even the concept "in the middle of" meant nothing. I drew some circles and said,

"These circles represent your friends standing around you. You are the X." The next day, I saw him walking across the playground with a group of boys. I walked over to him and whispered, "You are amid your friends." This boy lives in a ghetto area, has never known a stable home (is tossed from relative to relative), and I feel certain has no one who really talks with him about the things he sees or feels. On another day in group, we had to explore the concept of *beauty* with him. The other students contributed a "beautiful red rose," "a beautiful sunset," and a "beautiful woman" before he said, "You mean, like purple is a beautiful color?"

Visualization and verbalization activities are an effective way to foster concept development. When you locate an interesting sentence, put it on the chalkboard, ask the students to quietly reflect on it for a full minute, and then have them share their ideas and mental images in a group of four. Let one spokesperson from each group report to the class what went on in the group.

Words that have multiple meanings make the basis for many worthwhile lessons.

note—a short letter

note— ♪ in music

note—to notice

For follow-up activities (either orally or in writing), use these in different sentences so that the student must decide from the context of the sentence which meaning is being used. It is also important to help students learn to write sentences where the context of the sentence helps explain the meaning of the word. Example:

He wrote a note. (poor)

He wrote a note of thanks to his aunt for the gift she sent. (better)

The following words may be helpful in developing future lessons:

Words with multiple meanings	*Words that describe a concept*
can	What is a *vehicle?*
bolt	What is *crisp?* (find crisp things)

Words with multiple meanings	*Words that describe a concept*
bark	What is *enormous?* (relevant term—ultimately "something much bigger than whatever it's compared to")
cross	
calm	What is a *vegetable?*
club	What is *blond?* (When does it become brown?)
dash	What is *bravery?*
cover	What is *funny?* (They need to see its relevance—bring in a joke, cartoon, tell why it's funny to them.)
safe	
check	What is *stress?* (relevant—workaholic thrives on it; someone else breaks down under same conditions)
plain	
plug	
pit	
company	
fair	

My previous book, *How to Diagnose and Correct Learning Difficulties in the Classroom,* contains 77 activities for perceptual, conceptual, and language development. This book is available from Parker Publishing Company.

Note: Wherever possible, support discussions of word meaning with real objects or experiences.

TECHNIQUES FOR IMPROVING MEMORY

We have at least three kinds of memory, as follows:

1. Visual memory (memory for what we saw)
2. Auditory memory (memory for what we heard)
3. Kinesthetic memory (memory for what we did, felt, tasted, smelled).

Each of these kinds of memory has two forms: short term and long term.

When you see something or hear something, you have about 20 to 30 seconds to do something with it or it will be gone. When you look up a phone number and you're interrupted, you generally have to look it up again. You can move the phone number from your visual short-term memory to your longer-term memory by either repeating it several times (by so doing, you are supporting your visual short-term memory by coupling it in your auditory short-term memory) or by associating it with something you have already stored in your long-term memory. Even so, a week later you probably won't remember it. To retain it for longer periods, you must either use it often or be very motivated to remember it. Likewise, if you want to remember something you've heard, you may make notes on it to help remember it; but critical to transferring it to your long-term memory is using it. Most people must do something 90 times before they know it. Knowing this, we should be sure we give the student the 90 or more exposures he needs to learn a skill once he understands it.

Problem: Some students have long-term or short-term memory deficits.

Solution:

1. Use Selma E. Herr's auditory perceptual training exercises for improving memory.

2. Teach students to spell to the mastery level the words they use most frequently. Mastery has occurred when the child can spell a previously mastered list with 100% accuracy one month later without restudying). Likewise, if he consistently spells a given word correctly in his incidental writing, we can assume that he knows it.

3. Teach phonics—4 or 5 words are phonetically spelled so that if a child can learn to unblend a word such as *ch i l d* and can relate the correct symbol to each sound, he can spell well enuf to mak hmslf undrstd. (The basic purpose of a written note is communication.) If the spelling is close enough, modern technology will soon assist the learning disabled to spell correctly. (On the market already are typewriters with built-in spelling correctors.)

4. We need to teach students with poor memory how to use bypass techniques. For example, if after 3 years of trying to memorize the multiplication tables, the student is still having difficulties, we need to teach him to use a pocket calculator to support his math. He needs to be taught to be diligent, to keep the calculator near at hand and in good working order, and to double- or triple-check his answers.

5. Teach students to relate some familiar or known information to new information. For example, if the child has studied *vol*canoes in the past, the word meaning for re*vol*ution can be related—*vol*: "to blow up."

6. Teach students to use acronyms to help with spelling—for example, *A rat in the house might eat the ice cream* is the acronym for *arithmetic.*

7. Provide as many tactile experiences as you can.

I hear,
    and I forget.

I see,
    and I remember.

I do, and I understand.

An Ancient Chinese Proverb

8. The student's memory can sometimes be stimulated with a remark such as "Will I need to tell you this 90 times or will once be enough?" If the student says "once," he is making a commitment to try to remember. When students commit themselves to remember a point, they pay better attention and may indeed retain it, provided that daily opportunities to use it are planned. The expression "use it or lose it" is true. Relearning, however, takes place more quickly than initial learning.

TECHNIQUES FOR ASSISTING THE STUDENT WITH ATTENTION DEFICIT DISORDER

Problem: About 5 percent to 10 percent of the general population and a much higher percent of the learning-disabled population suffer from a condition called *Attention Deficit Disorder (ADD)*. Once thought to be a condition only of childhood, we now believe it is a lifelong problem and may account for the impulsive acts of persons who abuse others.

The symptoms of attention deficit are described in Chapter 1.

There appear to be three types of ADD:

1. A pseudo-type
2. True ADD with hyperactivity
3. True ADD without hyperactivity

In pseudo-ADD, the natural rambunctious behavior of childhood continues into later years, but these children respond positively when controls are eventually set and consistently enforced. A pseudo-ADD student can generally bring his behavior into tolerable limits within 6 months.

The student with true ADD with hyperactivity is in motion constantly; he is up and down, over and under, through his chair, and often talks incessantly. He says, "I forgot" a lot. He loses things. When he is around, other students find it hard to work.

The student with true ADD without hyperactivity is not so easy to spot. He may be a quiet fidgeter, or he may be an unfocused, lethargic sort. He also loses things and forgets a lot. He may put his head down, and day-dream a lot.

Solution:

1. Referral for medical evaluation and possible medication
2. Altering the child's environment

Discuss your observations with the parents. Discuss both solutions. Solicit the parents' concerns. Provide information. If the student is to be taken to a physician, it is desirable that a referral letter accompany him. You will need the parents' written permission to release information to the doctor.

SAMPLE OF REFERRAL LETTER

FROM: Joan Harwell, RS, Panacea School

RE: Jane Doe   DOB: 3/16/80

Jane has been identified and is being served as a learning-handicapped child.

_____Jane_____ is a student in our school. We are concerned about some behaviors we have seen _____Jane_____ display (symptoms suggest Attention Deficit Disorder).

1. Good days/bad days.
2. On a bad day, Jane is negativistic and oppositional—prone to profanity and fighting.
3. Attention span is limited to only a few seconds unless Jane is given one-to-one help.
4. Parent reports that Jane cannot sit through a meal without being up and down several times.
5. Intrusive with fellow students—resented by them.

If medication is prescribed, be assured that we will be happy to monitor its effectiveness and report back to you.

In order to counsel parents regarding a medical referral, the following information will be helpful to you. At this time, there is no medical test that will confirm that the student has ADD. It is diagnosed by its symptoms. Physicians usually do a complete physical exam (often including an electroencephalogram and blood and urine tests) to assure themselves that they are working with a healthy child since it is unwise to prescribe stimulant therapy to children who show any tendency toward epilepsy or who have liver or heart disease.

When medication is prescribed, it is usually prescribed on a trial basis (a trial period of 3 to 4 weeks).

Parents and teachers need to monitor and report the effects of the drug therapy to the physician. If the parent is concerned about the child, this concern should be relayed to the physician as soon as possible.

The drugs commonly prescribed include Ritalin (methylphenidate hydrochloride), Cylert (pemoline), Dexedrine, Tofranil, and Millarel. Usually the physician will start the child on a minimal dose. Upon introduction to the drug, a student may react with even greater hyperactivity initially or may become zombie-like. It generally takes 2 to 3 weeks to see what the true effect of the medication is going to be. Initially some students show insomnia, loss of appetite, stomachache, depression, or irritability. If the side effects are mild and the benefits are good, the physician will often ask the parents to continue the drug for a few weeks to see if the side effects subside. If they continue or worsen, an alternative drug may be prescribed.

Within the medical community, there is disagreement on whether or not students should take stimulant drugs on Saturday and Sunday. Some physicians say yes, others say no. What generally determines what occurs is how the parents feel about it—can they tolerate the behavior of the unmedicated child?

Many doctors suggest that children not take Ritalin in the summer. This break allows the body to mature normally—an earlier criticism was that Ritalin stunted growth.

Students on stimulant therapy need to be seen at least once a year by their physician for reevaluation of the dosage and for general status of health. Once the effective dosage is found (and this varies from student to student), the family should follow the physician's directions for its use. If the effectiveness changes (as children begin to grow), the dosage may need to be changed.

As previously noted, some students do not benefit from stimulant therapy, and some parents refuse to consider it. Therefore, the question arises of how to handle these students. The following suggestions are offered:

1. Keep the environment—home and school—as quiet, calm, and structured as possible.

2. Have the child adhere as closely as possible to the same daily schedule: rise at the same hour, mealtimes at the same hour, bedtime at the usual hour.

3. If changes in schedule are necessary, tell the child ahead of time if possible and explain what the new schedule will be.

4. Avoid long trips; when extended shopping is done, arrange for a babysitter and leave the child at home.

5. Insist on order—teach the child to remember where things are kept and insist that he put them there.

6. At school, this student needs a patient, nurturing, quiet teacher who is willing and able to give extra one-to-one attention.

7. The student needs to sit near the teacher—often a touch will settle him.

8. A carrel out of the traffic pattern, facing a wall, or in a corner limits distraction.

9. Extra time or shortened assignments are often necessary since this child takes longer to do his work. This may mean that the child will need to repeat a grade or two.

10. A study-buddy can help the student.

11. Social skills training by parents and teachers may help him to accept direction, to correct errors gracefully, and to have good manners.

12. If possible, avoid stress-producing situations; if unavoidable, help the child prepare for them and move through them.

13. Families need to provide the child with nonstressful regular exercise, such as playing soccer.

14. The amount of TV viewing should be limited to one hour a day (not the hour before bed), and the parents should choose programs of a nonviolent, quieter (perhaps humorous) nature.

15. Homework should be limited to 40 minutes (two 20-minute sessions) per day for grades 1 to 3; 60 minutes (two 30-minute sessions) per day for grades 4, 5, and 6; and 1½ hours a day in secondary school. If the student cannot do all the homework assigned, the parent may want to explain this to the teacher, finding out which papers have higher priority.

    If the student has an enormous amount of math to do, perhaps the parent can copy the problems. Then the student can do them. Likewise, on long reading assignments, the parent and student can alternate reading paragraphs. To focus the child's attention, the parent will need to ask frequent questions about the material and help the student make notes.

    Parents should be near to give assistance with homework. If a parent cannot remain calm, he should decline to help and explain why to the teacher. Hiring a private tutor may be a viable alternative.

16. Attention deficit students need strategies to overcome the "I forgot" syndrome. These may help:

    a. A pocket-size spiral notebook in which the student writes all assignments (the teacher should check them for correctness and completeness). This notebook can be used by the parent and the teacher for two-way communication.

    b. The student may need to make notes and wear a rubber band on his wrist until he completes the task he might forget.

    c. Belongings should bear the student's name, room number, and school so that they can be returned if they are found.

17. When giving directions, the direction-giver should ask the student to repeat the directions; if the student cannot do so, repeat the directions or write them down for him.

18. The student should be trained to reread his own work aloud before submitting it.

19. The student should be discouraged from doing 2 activities at a time, such as TV and homework; he also needs to be encouraged to finish one activity before moving on to the next.

20. The student's playmates should be chosen by the parents—quieter sorts with good judgment. Two hyperactive children can stimulate each other into a fevered pitch.

21. The hyperactive child or adult often finds peace in solo work—gardening or writing or just resting or lying quietly. If he's all keyed up, arrange for him to rest or sleep for a while.

If the medication route is successful, it is by far the easier solution from a purely management efficacy standpoint. Students often report that they feel better with medication than without, and parents generally report a significant improvement in the quality of their home life.

If medication is not successful or is not attempted, the student will surely not receive maximum benefit from his educational experiences. It is also almost always necessary for such a child to repeat a grade or two in order for him to complete his K to 12 education.

5

INTERVENTION
IN SPECIFIC
SUBJECT AREAS

TEACHING THE LD STUDENT PENMANSHIP

Writing is a complex skill that involves all three systems—input, integration, and output. It is also strongly dependent on developmental level. Many children arrive at kindergarten without the skills prerequisite to writing—scribbling, identifying shapes, recognizing likenesses and differences. They have not learned to color, cut, or paste. Their memory is untrained. (Adequate memory is essential to writing well because you must formulate in your head what you want to say and be able to hold it there long enough to get it onto paper.) For most children, therefore, first-year school activities need to revolve around learning these skills.

Some children arrive at kindergarten able to write their name, to paint representational paintings, and to color within lines. They cut, paste, and quote numerous nursery rhymes. Concepts such as *under, over, around, through, first, last,* and *middle* are understood.

As educators, we have to recognize the differences in these two very different groups of children and to provide first-year school experiences according to their developmental level.

Once a child has mastered these essential skills, he can begin to learn to write. Prior to that time, you are going to create frustration for both of you if you try to teach him to write.

Writing manuscript letters. Initially the student must be taught how to correctly hold the pencil and how to place his paper on his desk:

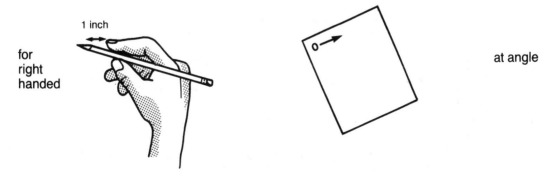

Most children have established dominance by kindergarten. To learn which hand students prefer, hand them ten small objects and observe which hand they usually use.

For children of cross-dominance (ambidextrous), begin with the hand of greater preference or the hand that produces the best-looking letters.

Some children do not know where to begin writing on a paper. To teach this, put a red dot and arrow on his paper, lightly in pencil. He begins just below the dot. ● moves ⟶ Erase the dot and arrow once he's started (see picture).

The student needs to be guided through making the letters. The teacher or parent helper demonstrates and talks him through each letter—showing him where to begin (tall letters such a *l* versus short letters such as *a*), which way to go, and so on (here is where the concepts of *up, down, around,* come into play). Allowing the child to trace over (on the chalkboard) the sample letters prior to paper writing is especially helpful.

An older student paired with each child is marvelous. The older student can watch to make sure that each letter is learned correctly.

When children begin to learn to write, they should work from a model. The model should not be dispensed with until you are sure that they are forming letters correctly by habit (not based on a single demonstration).

From the beginning, you will want to emphasize the concepts of one finger's space between each word, of being on line or under line, of clearly making sure that tall letters are tall and short letters are short.

A color-coded model of each letter is very helpful. These can be made on bristol board (heavy paper). A black dot signifies where the letter begins, the red line is the first stroke, a green line is the second stroke, and a blue line is for the third stroke if needed.

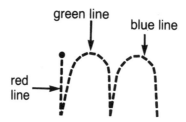

Letters of similar strokes are often taught together with a discussion about the common features; *c* becomes *a* or *d*, *e*. It is a short letter. Talk about the fact the *g*'s tail goes below the line.

> *a c d e g o q* (letters begin with same circle)
> versus
> *b h l t p k f* (tall letters)
> *m n r* (review height of bar "handle" *h n*)
> *u v w x y*
> *s z* (point out that *s* begins like a *c*)
> *i j*

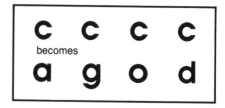

The student may need to practice the letter on the chalkboard. He writes it large. You, then, put a line under it so that he can see where the letter should be in relation to the line. When he returns to his paper, you talk him through the process. Say, "Think before you begin where the letter will begin, how far you have to move your pencil, and where you want to end up." (on the line).

Needless to say, it is more efficient and less frustrating to teach letter formation correctly at the start—even if you must go more slowly. Once a student has learned to make a letter incorrectly, it is very difficult—almost impossible—to teach him the correct way. If the child is past grade 3, I do not even attempt to change it. It is too frustrating for all concerned.

Once a child writes all his uppercase and lowercase letters correctly, you can move on to teaching him how to write words.

Children who are very dysgraphic will need to be introduced early to the computer and typewriter. It is unwise to harangue a child about his penmanship. He may lack the motor control necessary to produce legible letters.

Legibility is the real test of penmanship. Adequate expression of thoughts should remain our primary goal.

Cursive handwriting. It is customary to introduce cursive handwriting in grade 3. If a child has not mastered printing and reading, it is unwise to move him on to cursive. He needs to continue to print. However, there are times when you must let the child move on—for some children, disallowing it would damage their self-esteem. These children need one-to-one supervision by a cross-age tutor so that they can learn to correctly form individual letters and to correctly join letters to form words.

TEACHING THE LD STUDENT TO READ

Most children learn to read no matter what approach is used—cloze, phonics, whole language, or sight-say, but for one in seven children, reading does not come easily. *Dyslexic* is the term sometimes used to describe these children.

What is Dyslexia?	Common Symptoms
Dyslexia is a difference in brain formation which is present at birth and occurs in 15% of the general population. It results in an impairment in the ability to learn, retain, and express information. Recognition and manipulation of symbols, especially letters and numbers in sequence, present the most universal problem. One who is dyslexic, although of average or superior intelligence, may find difficulty in fol-	Childhood: • Difficulty expressing oneself • Delay in learning tasks such as tying shoes and telling time • Inattentiveness; distractibility • Inability to follow directions • Left-right confusion • Difficulty learning the alphabet, times tables, words of songs or rhymes • Poor playground skills • Difficulty learning to read

lowing directions, keeping track of possessions, finding the way without getting lost, and being aware of time. Memory and retention of newly learned information is often affected. Some dyslexics have difficulty with co-ordination, confusion of right and left, and impaired depth perception. The resulting tension contributes to a lower performance level in school tasks. Reading, writing, and math when taught in a traditional method can be difficult, if not impossible, for the dyslexic to master.

Dyslexia continues throughout life. Without early diagnosis, special reme-diation and the teaching of coping skills, it can result in a severe loss of self-esteem, limited friendships, and failure in school and career pursuits.

- Mixing the order of letters or num-bers while writing

Adolescence and Adulthood:
- Difficulty in processing auditory in-formation
- Losing possessions; poor organiza-tional skills
- Slow reading; low comprehension
- Difficulty remembering names of people and places
- Hesitant speech; difficulty finding appropriate words
- Difficulty organizing ideas to write a letter or paper
- Poor spelling
- Inability to recall numbers in proper sequence
- Lowered self-esteem due to past frus-trations and failures

Reprinted with the permission of the Orton Dyslexia Society, P.O. Box 4263, Irvine, CA 92716.

I am very reluctant to use the label *dyslexic*, because of public ignorance. To some, this label means "hopeless" or "can't learn." With early diagnosis, special remediation, and coping skills, dyslexic children can and do learn.

The reading program outlined in this section has worked well for me. It produces results quickly, it is easy to follow, and it requires no costly materials.

Sequentially you teach the following:

1. Consonant and short vowel sounds
2. Blending (reading word attack) and unblending (spelling)
3. Sight words
4. Special combinations as they occur—*sh, th, oo, ou, ow, ing, all*, etc.
5. Rules for short or long vowels and other rules for structural analysis
6. New vocabulary
7. Related reading skills

When you begin working with a new student, you want to inspire confidence in him so that you'll be able to teach him where others have failed. You might say, "I have some magic I'll share with you."

Teaching the Young Student

> The first IEP goal would say "____[student name]____ will give a correct sound for all alphabet letters except *y*."

If the student has acquired few or no sounds from prior instruction, this process usually takes about 20 consecutive days. The longest it has ever taken was 40 days.

You may work with one student at a time (30 minutes daily), but it is possible to work with up to four beginning students at a time. It is necessary to give adequate blending and feedback time to each student. This individual feedback is absolutely critical.

Either on the chalkboard, on a sheet of paper (which all four students can see), or on a ditto (given to each student), draw each alphabet letter. (See form on following page.)

Say: "The letter's name is *a*. Repeat, please." Be sure that the students repeat, "The letter's name is *a*" rather than just saying "*a*".

Say: "The letter's sound is _____." (Give the short *a* sound.) Simultaneously, draw an apple on the chalkboard or on their paper. If you're working with a group, they can draw their own apple. Do not allow them to say, "The letter's sound is *apple*."

Say: "*Apple* is a word that starts with _____ [again make the short *a* sound— really overemphasize it], but it takes five letters to spell *apple*." Write *apple*, point, and count to the five letters, then repeat, "The letter's sound is _____."

Say: "The letter's name is *b*. Repeat, please." (pause) "The sound of *b* is _____." Be sure not to say "buh." *B* is just a pursing of the lips and a tiny amount (puff) of air. It is not a vocalized sound. If students say, "buh," teach them to make a pure *b* by watching your lips. If they are allowed to say "buh," it will become a problem in blending—*bat* comes out "buh-at," so the child doesn't hear a word he recognizes. He knows what a *bat* is but not a *buh-at*.

Say: "*B* is the sound you hear in ball." Write *ball*. Draw a ball. Say, "How many letters did it take to spell *ball*?" Help them count.

Say: "The letter's name is *c*. It says _____." (Make the sound of *c* as in *car*. Again, be sure to say a pure *k* sound—not *kuh*. Do not mention at this point that *c* has two sounds. The student will learn that later.)

Say: "The letter's name is *c*. Its sound is _____." Write *car*, draw a car. "How many letters are in *car*? Count them."

Say: "The letter's name is *d*. Its sound is _____." (Make the sound of *d*, draw a door, write *door*.) Be careful not to say "duh." *D*, like *b*, is just a little air against the teeth.

Say: "Let's see, *apple* has five letters, *ball* has four, *car* has three, *door* has four. Different words have a different number of letters. We put sounds together to get words."

Say: "The letter's name is *e*. The sound of *e* is _____." (Make the sound you hear in *Ed*.) Raise your hands above your head. Say, "I call *e* the hands-up sound. I'll explain why in a minute."

a j s

b k t

c l u

d m v

e n w

f o x

g p y

h q u z

i r

Say: "The letter's name is *f*. The sound of *f* is _____." (Make the sound of *f* as in *fish*.) Ask them to repeat the letter's name and sound.

Say: "The letter's name is *g*. It's sound is _____." (Make the sound of *g* in *go*.) Write *go*. Unblend *g o* so that the children can hear two sounds. Raise one finger as you make the *g* sound, raise a second finger as you make the *o* sound. "Did you hear both sounds?" Unblend it again raising one, then two fingers as you do.

Say: "The letter's name is *h*. *H* says _____. This is the sound you hear in *house*. [Be sure it's just air, not "huh."] Repeat."

Say: "The letter's name is *i*. It says _____." (Make the sound you hear in the word *is* or *it*.) "I call this the hands-down sound. Listen to the difference between the sound of *e* and *i* as I say them." Raise your hands, say "*e*" (as in *Ed*). Put your hands in your lap and say "*i*" (as in *is* and *it*).*

It is absolutely imperative that the child learn to hear the subtle differences in these vowel sounds. A child may need to learn to watch how far he opens his mouth. It's wide open like biting an apple for *a*; it's not open as far for an *e*—his mouth should look like this with his teeth resting gently on each side of his finger.

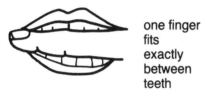

one finger
fits
exactly
between
teeth

You may need to have him look in a mirror, practicing *e* as he says *Ed*.

When he makes the "*i*" sound as in *it*, his lips and teeth can almost touch.

Proceed on with the other letters. When you get to *o*, say, "*O* is the sound you hear in *octopus* or the sound you make when the doctor tells you to open your mouth and say, "A-hh."

When you teach *p*, be sure that they purse their lips, blowing more air than for *b*. Let them feel the difference as you make *b* and *p* (place the palm of their hand in front of your mouth as you say "b"). "This is a *b* [puff]. Now here's a *p* [harder puff]. Can you feel the difference? You have to blow a *p* out." On the ditto, I draw ⟨p⟩ . The three rays mean lots of air.

Say: "The letter's name is *q*. *Q* is a very shy fellow. He never goes anywhere without *u*. *Qu* says _____." (Make the *kw* sound as in *queen*.) Repeat.

Say: "The letter's name is *r*. *R* says _____." (Make the *er* sound as in *her*.) Sometimes I say, "Er, er, er" and then say, "It's the sound a car makes when it won't start."

_____

*The tactile cue of hands-up or hands-down seems to be very helpful to children. I'm not sure why. Likewise, the finger between the lips for the *e* is often the only way that children with auditory discrimination difficulties can learn the correct sound of *e*.

Say: "The letter's name is *s*. S says _____." (Be sure that the child doesn't say "sh.") The teeth are almost closed, the air comes, hits the front incisor area, and escapes.

After you have gone through all the letters of the alphabet, it is important to help them see that by putting letters together, we get words.

On the first day,

I make the sound of the *a* pointing to the *a*, and then I make the sound of the *t* while pointing to it. I say the sounds quicker and quicker until the child hears *at* not a . . t.

Next I say and write a sentence, as follows:

> We are at school. (I ask them to locate the *at* and circle it.)

Next we do

The sentence I say and write is, "Just as I came in, the phone rang." They find and circle the word *as*.

Next we do

The sentence I say and write is, "Go ask your mom if you can go."

When you finish each day, the student worksheet should look like the one on the next page.

The referents for

j is jar

k is kite

l is lamp

m is moon

n is nose

u is up

v is vase

y is omitted at this point. Y is the only letter with 3 sounds: y = you, yes

y = "e" happy, baby

y = "i" my, try

You will find that LD children quickly learn the sounds for letters that have only one sound. Their confusion occurs with letters that have two or three sounds (*a*, *e*, *i*, *o*, *u*, *y*, *c*, *g*).

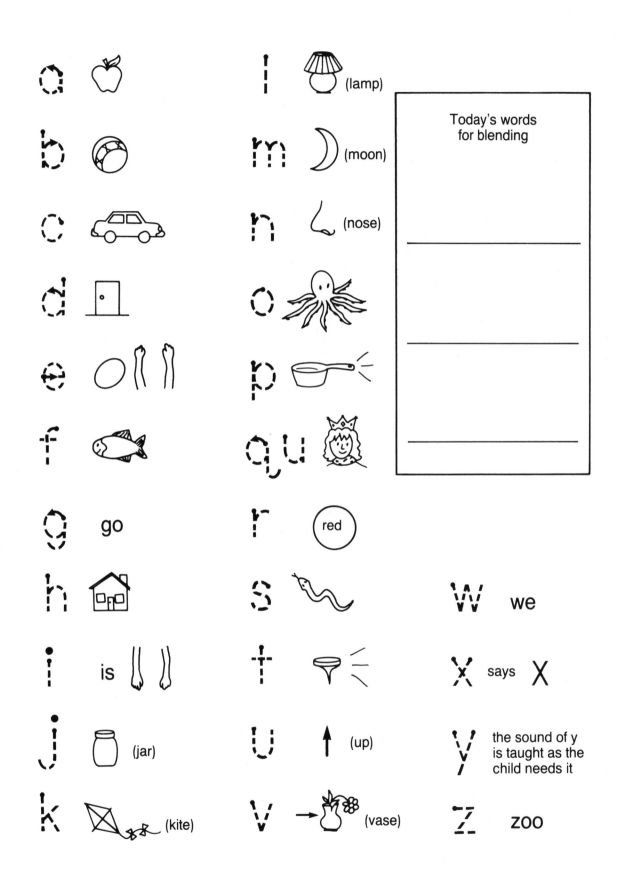

a (apple)

b (ball)

c (car)

d (door)

e (egg/legs)

f (fish)

g go

h (house)

i is (legs)

j (jar)

k (kite)

l (lamp)

m (moon)

n (nose)

o (octopus)

p (pan)

qu (queen)

r red

s (snake)

t (top)

u (up)

v (vase)

w we

x says X

y the sound of y is taught as the child needs it

z zoo

Today's words
for blending

_____

_____

_____

Each day we go through the whole list writing the letter correctly, saying its name and sound, and drawing the referent. It is essential to this program that the referents are always the same. Even if the child does not draw well, he will soon catch on that *l* is always a lamp, *m* is always a moon, and so on.

Each day we also do some blending. We use two-, three-, and four-letter words with short *a, o, u* (easily discriminated vowels). Later when the child is proficient with *a, o, u*, you can add *e, i* words.

At first you'll need to help him blend. It is imperative to get the first two sounds together—*ca* (pause) *p* rather than *c* (pause) *ap*.

Here is a list of *a, o, u* words that you can use:

hug	cut	jug	pal	tax	cast
up	tuck	mob	pat	clad	hunt
on	cot	brag	plot	bulb	fat
am	crab	bud	plug	wax	log
as	slam	dot	plan	raft	cost
off	pup	ham	tug	rap	top
bug	rub	flat	loft	fad	fast
us	fond	not	hog	cram	fun
full	mat	box	back	lad	jump
hot	lamp	bus	dog	dug	stop
rut	fan	has	frog	job	dull
at	bag	nap	glad	hat	rob
cat	had	man	lost	band	rot
can	but	sun	soft	last	pull
and	doll	fox	put	long	snap
map	fact	tan	slap	grab	sad
ask	egg	flag	bank	map	past
gum	ran	pat	cup	spot	hop
bad	mad	tub	tag	run	camp
gun	wag	jam	pot	trap	lot
rug	rat	jog	scan	dad	slot
nut	mud	lack	drum		

As you are teaching, help the child to realize that if you change even one letter, you've changed the word. Insist that he look carefully and compare how words are alike or different. Words such as *can, cat, cap* illustrate how the final consonant changes the word. Students must realize that changing one letter changes the word. Words such as *got, hot,* and *rot* illustrate the importance of the initial consonant. Words such as *bag, beg, big, bog,* and *bug* illustrate what changing a vowel can do.

When a child is blending, he may have a hard time hearing what he is saying. If he sings the sounds or whispers the sounds, it may help. Otherwise you need to model how the sounds should slowly blend together. When you feel that the students are reasonably proficient with *a, o, u*, add *e, i* words, such as the following:

in	set	rib	best	let	fed
is	sit	men	gift	pet	sled
it	sell	tip	fit	tell	slid
if	elm	pen	hen	fix	rid
hit	lift	get	wet	fill	beg
did	left	lint	fell	will	net
help	send	mess	belt	grin	bit
lip	kill	red	felt	kick	big
leg	clip	yes	milk	dip	peg
hid	ten	yet	miss	lick	pig
neck	spin	bed	list	sick	wig
web					

As you begin to work on all five short vowels, you will want to simultaneously teach the student to spell all the words that he will encounter in the first story of his first reader (in the reader that we use, there are nine). In the section on spelling techniques, you will find ways to teach these. When I am absolutely sure that the child can spell all the words in the first story, then I hand him the book for the first time. If he stumbles on a word, I say, "What letters do you see?" As he names them, he will recall from his spelling activities what the word is. He feels successful!

The procedure is the same for each story in his first text—he must be able to spell all the words before he reads the story. We spend lots of time decoding and doing spelling activities. This means that your progress will be slow at the start, but it will pay off. It's like a train's movements—very slow at first, but the train gains speed as it gains power. Likewise, the student gains speed as he becomes proficient at phonetic and structural analysis.

The reading series we use is accompanied by a Skillpak. This Skillpak can be used to provide spelling activities as well as reading activities. If there is a picture of an object that can be spelled phonetically, you can draw enough lines and encourage the child to spell the word. Likewise, if there is a picture for which the child can write a simple sentence, help him to do so. (See sample lesson at the end of this section.)

At this point, the child must learn to say, "The vowels are *a e i o u*— and sometimes *y* and *w*." He must be taught that every word has at least one vowel.

Be alert for the introduction of the two-vowel rule. I have found that the rhyme "When two vowels go walking, the first one does the talking" means nothing to children. What does work is to tell them about "the bully." For example, *r a n* spells *ran*, but if you add another vowel, as in rain, the *i* (the bully) reaches over and tells the *a*, "You had better say your name, not *a* as in *apple*." This is why you spent all those days having the child repeat, "The letter's name is *a*; its sound is _____ (as in *apple*)."

At first the child will need daily practice applying this rule. The following words are particularly helpful:

can	*becomes*	cane	The *a* has a long $\bar{a}$
hop		hope	sound because of the
us		use	second vowel.
cap		cape	
hat		hate	
kit		kite	
fed		feed	
bed		bead	
slid		slide	
pin		pine	
met		meet	
rid		ride	
strip		stripe	
got		goat	
rob		robe	
cut		cute	
men		mean	
set		seat	
dim		dime	
cot		coat	
red		read	
rip		ripe	
bit		bite	

Be alert for the introduction of what I call "peanut-butter" sounds; for the *th* , the tongue must come out; *sh* (the same noise you make when telling someone to be quiet); *ch* ; *ph* (f). Teach *ou/ow, oo, ing, al/all, ar, er/ir/ur, au/aw, oi/oy, ew, or,* as they occur in reading.

When you put peanut butter on bread, if you try to pull it off, the bread tears—just so, these letters are stuck together and have unique new sounds.

As each combination is introduced, give the child daily practice, using it by making lists of words and having him decode them or learn to spell them. The *EDL Core Vocabulary*[3] book is indispensable because it will help you make lists quickly.

Be alert to teach the rules that help a child with the sound of *c*, *g*.

C always says "k" unless it is followed by *e*, *i*, *y*—then it will always say "s."

G usually says "g" as in *go* unless it is followed by *e*, *i*, *y*—then it may say *j* as in *age*.

I refer to *e*, *i*, *y* as the bad boys. "*C*'s mom doesn't like for him to run around with *e*, *i*, *y* because when he does, he talks nasty, hissing at people."

In your reading of series, be alert for the introduction of the syllabication rules vc/cv or vc/ccv. In this case, the word breaks between the first and second consonants. The break is like a brick wall, preventing the next vowel from making the first vowel say its name.   t e m / p̂ l e.   Remember that peanut-butter sounds such as *th* count as one consonant and cannot be separated, thus *al   though* is a vc/cv word

al/*tho*
‖ ‖
vc/cv

The o cannot get over the brick wall to kick the *a*.

Teaching the Older Student

If I get a student who is reading at grade 2.0 or better, I do not use the procedure for beginning students. I do try to locate and remediate the student's deficit areas. There are three primary offenders. First, I check to see if he knows the two sounds for each vowel and how to apply the one-vowel (short sound) and two-vowel rule (long sound). Second, I check to see that he understands how to syllabicate vc/cv or vc/ccv words. Third, I watch to learn which combinations he needs help on. Using the EDL vocabularies, it is then possible to develop lists to meet his specific deficit areas.

You may need to spend 2 to 3 months teaching decoding skills before putting a student in a reader. This time is not wasted, for when you do assign a reader, it will be a higher-level book, and he will feel less defeated and more successful.

In working with older students, you may find that the following list of nonsense words is very helpful when you are trying to locate deficit areas or trying to teach decoding rules. It allows you to know whether students are decoding or guessing.

List of Nonsense Syllables

lait	mercod	ug	codflet	stope
exnig	motwog	dand	rimegrab	coise
deline	fash	knise	telejar	shight
thig	tim lab sep	ait	itpag	mose
ut	aig	peet	tabe	tud

---

[3]Standord E. Taylor and others, *EDL Core Vocabularies in Reading, Mathematics, Science, and Social Studies,* EDL, 2 Park Avenue, New York, NY 10016 (copyright 1979, McGraw-Hill, Inc.)

STUDENTS' REMINDER FOR DECODING

Rule 1 ——► When you come to a new word
Count the vowels

If 1,   a =   e =   i = is

o =   u = ↑

Rule 2 ——► If 2 or more, look for vc/cv
vc/ccv

Otherwise: a⌢lone

Rule 3 ——► Watch for special combinations

sh =   also ci often
                             ti   say sh

ch = or k

Th =

ph = f

er   her
ir   girl
ur   burn

or = for

ar =

ew = new

wr = w̸r

kn = k̸n

gh = ghost
night
laugh
f

ci sometimes says sh as in special

oo = too

ing = thing

ou = out

ow { now
     snow

tion/sion = shun

al = all

oi/oy = boy

au/aw = saw

y = yes
    my (i)
    happy (e)

c = k

ce
ci } always
cy   say
      S

g = go

ge
gi } sometimes
gy   say
      J

© 1989 by The Center for Applied Research in Education

len	talmy	reak	eljon	zab
nutwel	ralty	perjan	hoy	twil
rosine	pel	sloap	sipnol	aglib
belfit	kips	polykud	chenning	libetoge
lumdy	prot	grube	comrile	exmal
telecab	het	swade	givfamshid	wagleb
shil	gib	extaim	anti leep blad	mook
sieen	crad	conwasion	gof hick	soe
untag	lout	treap	adfloit	leat
cotly	teed	tum dag	perlap	bot
knos	itshom	sook	grize	loice
magsib	saft	reg	naip	fets
lifbet	pook	thoud	rabe	thibe
agsub	dight	pight	linning	wim
quif	ston	goy	jash	snik
bandy	bleem	qued	polylug	confation
ep	glat	zan	stope	labbing
skiep	sode	lidgas		

With the older student, be certain that the student's vocabulary development and general information fund are adequate to support his reading. If you have given a Woodcock Reading Test, you will want to locate reading material that is in his comfortable reading grade level or his easy-reading level. Never assign a student to a book that is at his failure reading level. Remember: Start low, go slow!

For the older student, the series called *Multiple Skills* (Barnell-Loft, 1978) is excellent. It has the following advantages:

1. Stories are short—one-half page each.

2. New words introduced are repeated and reinforced and occur again shortly.

3. Many skills are taught—finding the main idea, scanning for information, inferential thinking, and vocabulary development.

4. The material spans a wide range of interest.

Teaching New Vocabulary

The most effective way that I have found for teaching new vocabulary involves making matching cards. You will also need to make a ditto to accompany the cards. (Put the child's name on so that you can return lost cards. The 9 means that this is his ninth word list.)

Bill—9
word

Bill—9
definition (write in red ink)

Fifteen words make a good list (30 card total). By color-coding definition cards in red, the child can quickly sort piles of words and piles of meanings. He places definition cards on his desk, you shuffle word cards, and he matches pairs (word and its definition) daily until he can do it 100% for three to four days. He needs an accompanying ditto for all fifteen words that gives the word, the definition, and a sentence using the word to help him in the initial stages. For example:

1. *Keen*—clever, smart, sharp, She has a *keen* mind and catches on quickly.

Following directions.   Crucial to becoming a good student is learning how to read and understand directions.

1. Teach the student to place stop signs wherever there is a period or a question mark.

In each sentence below, you will find an underlined word. From the list below, select a word that means the same or almost the same as the underlined word. Write the word on the blank.   When you are done, there will be three words left over.

wrath	swiftly	common	verge	billow
blustery	controlled	calmly	contain	capture

We had never seen the boat move so *fast*.

---

2. Have the student read to the first stop sign. You repeat a portion of the sentence to him. "In each sentence below"—stop and ask, "What do they mean by *below?*" Wait for the student to find the sentence that begins with, "We had never seen . . ."

3. The student reads, "You will find an underlined word." Stop and say, "Show me the underlined word." Wait until he points to the word *fast*.

4. Continue until he can read directions.

   It takes about fifteen lessons to teach a student how to read directions. (Students will need to be reminded to practice this skill on succeeding days or they will forget what to do.) Students should be told that the purpose of the lesson is to learn to read directions. LD students need to follow through on completing the first direction before going on to others. (If they read all directions and then try to do what was said, they'll usually leave out some part.)

Paraphrasing.   Paraphrasing is an important skill to teach. Initially it is a way for us to check the student's comprehension of a passage. Later it will serve as a basis for notetaking.

When a student paraphrases, he puts the meaning of the passage into his own words.

In the process of paraphrasing, most people weed out the trivia, extracting the essence. For example, the paragraph says:

> The table was laden with all sorts of good things to
> eat—beans, sweet potatoes, salad. A fine, large brown turkey
> was the centerpiece, and all eyes were on it as Dad carved the
> first slice. A wave of thankfulness and an appreciation of
> our state of well-being flooded over me.

paraphrased it says:

> It was Thanksgiving Day, and I felt good.

The question arises: "When should paraphrasing begin?" The answer is, "The earlier the better." It can begin at age 4 or 5 as students listen to stories being read to them. They can be asked questions about the story—to summarize the story and to put the events of the story in sequence.

Certainly as soon as students read the first story to you, it is essential that you ask them to explain what happened. Beginning to check understanding at this early stage will ensure that students do not become so involved in decoding that they are not in tune with the real purpose of reading—communication.

If the student is older when he first comes to you, and diminished comprehension is one of his weaknesses, it may be that he has never been routinely asked to paraphrase and summarize. He will need to be taught these skills.

Paraphrasing often reveals errors in the student's understanding. For example, an early story in the reading series we use (Ginn 720) has to do with some children who are putting on a play at school. The play is a depiction of the nursery rhyme, "Hey diddle, diddle, the cat and the fiddle, the cow jumped over the moon."

I find that LD students have often never been in a play, never seen a play, and their only concept of *play* is the recreational playing they do. Many do not know the nursery rhyme, and they make no connection between the story and the name of their book, *The Little Dog Laughed*. When you ask them to paraphrase what is happening in the story, these deficits become evident when you ask, "What happened in the story?" They answer, "I don't know." Having children participate in a play is the quickest way for them to learn about plays. (Use a story well-known to them, such as the "Three Billy Goats Gruff.")

Paraphrasing can be integrated with a regular reading lesson. As the child reads in his text, he can be asked "What was that story about?". Paraphrasing can also be taught as a skill—in isolation from other skills. You can make and use cards to teach this skill.

Here are some sample cards to teach paraphrasing as a skill (in isolation). Have the student read the card and then answer the question orally. The answer can be given in 2 to 10 words.

Blue sky. Puffy white clouds. Gentle breezes blow.

"What kind of day is it?"
(Answer in less than 5 words.)

The sound of a siren could be heard in the distance. I ran outside to see what was going on. Smoke and flames shot from the roof of the house across the street.

"What is happening?"

(Answer in less than 5 words.)

My stomach and head hurt. My throat was so sore I could barely swallow. Mother said I could not go to school. I did not feel like it anyway. I stayed in bed all day and slept.

"What is going on?"

(Answer in 5 words.)

I flapped my arms. I kicked my legs. I held my breath. I sank under the water sometimes, but I kept on trying.

"What was he trying to do?"

(Answer in 7 words or less.)

The bus was waiting. The children were jumping up and down. They had swimsuits, sand pails, and lunch boxes. The teacher said that they could get on the bus.

"What's happening?"

(Answer in 10 words or less.)

Sam could not sleep. Spelling words kept running through his head. He had talked his mom into giving him a dime for each 100% he made. He had eight dimes.

"What's happening?"

(Answer in 10 words or less.)

Recognizing fact from opinion. Another important skill is teaching children to separate fact from opinion. The quickest way to do this is to teach children to recognize the following words that always signal an opinion statement:

like/hate	boring/interesting
think	relaxing
wonder	good/bad
pretty	believe
nice	feel
beautiful	easy/hard
delicious	should
wonderful	feel
fun	seems

This makes a good ongoing chart activity. Hang a chart with the title "Opinion Words," and let students add words whenever they come across new ones. Anytime someone adds a word, it is a good time for a mini-review. Emphasize that a fact is a statement that can be proved or disproved to the satisfaction of all and an opinion is a statement that one person agrees with while another may totally disagree.

General Principles for Reading

Beginning readers need to read aloud. Insist on accuracy. Have them reread sentences until they are fluent. At the end of the story, ask them to summarize the major events of the story—properly sequencing them.

If a Skillpak is involved, look ahead at the test and prepare them for the test. You can help students get high scores by making sure that they thoroughly know and can use the vocabulary words that will be tested. Be sure that they are proficient on the word attack skills that will be tested. Make sure to give practice items in the same format as the test.

As a student's reading level becomes more fluent and he reaches grade 2.5 to 3.0, you may want to pair students for reading. Let them read alternate paragraphs or pages to one another. (The one not reading keeps the other honest.) You should circulate among the pairs, listening, giving help, making sure that they are insisting on meaning from what they have read.

Encourage recreational reading. Read to them. Have books available that are high interest/low vocabulary. Reward recreational reading. Book reports should be given orally. Most LD students balk at the idea of the written report. Encourage parents to read to their child.

At the beginning of this chapter, I mentioned that there are several systems for teaching reading. I strongly believe that for most learning-disabled students, a sound program for reading involves the use of a combination of all four approaches.

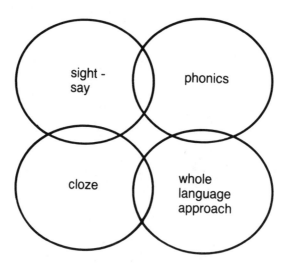

Our language contains over 500,000 words. It is not possible for any brain to store and retrieve that many words. Phonics is a system for reducing larger words to a workable number of component parts. Approximately four out of five words can be decoded with phonics. For the remaining words, we need to teach students to use cloze and sight-say techniques. I refer to words such as *busy* as "crazy" words. They are words that do not follow rules but that need to be well taught. Cloze involves having a student use the context of the sentence to help him make sense out of the "crazy" words. Sight-say involves simply memorizing the word using its configuration to assist.

In the whole language approach, the emphasis is on teaching children to enjoy reading—to seek out the ideas and to recognize the artful style of the author. Children are encouraged to write their own stories and to develop an appreciation for subtle nuance of each word.

In the language experience approach, the student tells his story while the teacher writes it. Then the student learns to read it back. This approach has value since it allows students to become acquainted with the words that they actually use in daily speech.

In this chapter, I have told you how I teach reading. There are several other fine programs available that work well for LD students. The Open Court Correlated Language Program (Open Court Publishers, 315 Fifth Street, Peru, IL 61354) published in 1971 and the Orton-Gillingham approach (Orton Dyslexia Society, 724 York Road, Baltimore, MD 21204) are both good phonics-based programs. For learning-disabled students, I believe that phonics is a necessity. I have heard it said that some LD kids cannot learn phonics. I do not believe that. I do believe that some phonics programs are so poorly constructed that LD students have not made the necessary connection between phonics and reading.

SAN BERNARDINO CITY UNIFIED SPECIAL EDUCATION LOCAL PLAN AREA
INDIVIDUALIZED EDUCATION PROGRAM — PART II

NAME __Doe, Jane__   BIRTHDATE __3-16-81__

DATE __3-7-89__

Short Term Objectives	Person(s) Responsible For Implementation *	Hours Per Week **	Methods, Materials and Activities	Evaluation
By __6-15-89__ , the student will demonstrate an increased competency in GOAL — _word attack_ OBJ _Given 20 words with short vowels (CVC, VC), Jane will orally decode them w 80% acc. (3 trials)_	_Rsp_	_1-5 total_	_2X weekly practice_	Achieved _____ Not Achieved _____ METHODS OF MEASUREMENT ☐ Observer ■ Teacher Made Test ☐ Standardized Test ☐ CR Test ☐ Other _____
By __2-28-90__ , the student will demonstrate an increased competency in GOAL — _word attack_ OBJ _Given 50 wds with short/long vowel sounds at gr 2 difficulty Jane will orally decode them w 80% acc_	_Rsp_	_";_	_Words taken from EDL Core Voc. and 2nd gr. texts_	Achieved _____ Not Achieved _____ METHODS OF MEASUREMENT ☐ Observer ■ Teacher Made Test ☐ Standardized Test ☐ CR Test ☐ Other _____
By __6-15-89__ , the student will demonstrate an increased competency in GOAL — _main idea_ OBJ _Jane will orally read a gr 1.5-1.9 text and answer the criterion test questions w 80% acc_	_Rsp_	_";_	_Ginn 720 "Across the Fence" or related materials from another series_	Achieved _____ Not Achieved _____ METHODS OF MEASUREMENT ☐ Observer ☐ Teacher Made Test ☐ Standardized Test ■ CR Test ☐ Other _____
By __2-28-90__ , the student will demonstrate an increased competency in GOAL — _main idea_ OBJ _Jane will orally read a gr 2.0-2.4 text and answer the criterion test questions w 80% acc_	_"_	_";_	_Ginn 720 "Glad to Meet you" or similar series_	Achieved _____ Not Achieved _____ METHODS OF MEASUREMENT ☐ Observer ☐ Teacher Made Test ☐ Standardized Test ☐ CR Test ☐ Other _____
By __6-15-89__ , the student will demonstrate an increased competency in GOAL — _Spelling_ OBJ _When the Dolch pre primer wds (B3) are dictated Jane will write them w 100% acc_	_"_	_";_	_color coding, configuration, play spelling activities 2-3X weekly_	Achieved _____ Not Achieved _____ METHODS OF MEASUREMENT ☐ Observer ■ Teacher Made Test ☐ Standardized Test ☐ CR Test ☐ Other _____

SE-51 (Rev. 7/87)   This is not a contract for services   White — Program Supervisor or District Office   Canary — Teacher   Pink — Parent   Goldenrod — Cum File   Circle all revisions of IEP with date and parent, teacher and administrator's initials

135

SAN BERNARDINO CITY UNIFIED SPECIAL EDUCATION LOCAL PLAN AREA
INDIVIDUALIZED EDUCATION PROGRAM — PART II

NAME: Doe, Jane BIRTHDATE 3-16-81

DATE 3-7-89

Short Term Objectives	Person(s) Responsible For Implementation *	Hours Per Week **	Methods, Materials and Activities	Evaluation
By 12-15-89 the student will demonstrate an increased competency in: GOAL — Spelling OBJ: When the Dolch pre-primer/primer (8b) words are dictated, Jane will spel (write) them w 100% acc	Rap	1-5 total	see previous statement of act.	Achieved __ Not Achieved __ METHODS OF MEASUREMENT ☐ Observer ■ Teacher Made Test ☐ Standardized Test ☐ CR Test ☐ Other __
By 2-28-90 the student will demonstrate an increased competency in: GOAL — spelling OBJ: When the Dolch grl wds are dictated, Jane will write them w 100% acc	"	"		Achieved __ Not Achieved __ METHODS OF MEASUREMENT ☐ Observer ■ Teacher Made Test ☐ Standardized Test ☐ CR Test ☐ Other __
By 12-15-89 the student will demonstrate an increased competency in: GOAL — writing sentences OBJ Jane will write 5-10 sentences each week. Each will have a noun (subject), verb, phrase. All errors to be corrected under supervision	Rap *"	"	beg Sept 89	Achieved __ Not Achieved __ METHODS OF MEASUREMENT ☐ Observer ☐ Teacher Made Test ☐ Standardized Test ☐ CR Test ■ Other __Sample
By 2-28-90 the student will demonstrate an increased competency in: GOAL — writing sentences OBJ Without help Jane will write 5 sentences. Each will be grammatically correct mechanically correct. Fewer than 3 spelling errors	"	"		Achieved __ Not Achieved __ METHODS OF MEASUREMENT ☐ Observer ☐ Teacher Made Test ☐ Standardized Test ☐ CR Test ■ Other __Sample
By 2-28-90 the student will demonstrate an increased competency in: GOAL — Subtraction OBJ: Given 10 subtraction problems (incl. 4 story problems) w/ and w/o regrouping - ex _80_ _97_ -39 or -23 Jane will write the answers w 80% acc	Rap *"	1-5 total	beg Sept 89 2-3x weekly practice	Achieved __ Not Achieved __ METHODS OF MEASUREMENT ☐ Observer ■ Teacher Made Test ☐ Standardized Test ☐ CR Test ☐ Other __

SE-51 (Rev. 7/87) This is not a contract for services White — Program Supervisor or District Office Canary — Teacher Pink — Parent Goldenrod — Cum File Circle all revisions of IEP with date and parent, teacher and administrator's initials

NAME __Doe, Jane__

BIRTHDATE __3-16-81__

DATE __3 - 3 - 89__

Short Term Objectives	Person(s) Responsible For Implementation*	Hours Per Week**	Methods, Materials and Activities	Evaluation
By __2-28-90__ , the student will demonstrate an increased competency in: GOAL — __multiplication__ OBJ __Given 20 simple multiplication prob. ex. 6x3 or xy, Jane will demonstrate she understands the concept by illustrating and finding the answers__	__Rap.__	__1-5 total__	__Activities this page__ __beg. Sept 89__ $6 \times 3 = 18$ ⦿ ⦿ ⦿ ⦿ ⦿ ⦿	Achieved _____ Not Achieved _____ **METHODS OF MEASUREMENT** ☐ Observer ▣ Teacher Made Test ☐ Standardized Test ☐ CR Test ☐ Other __80% acc__
By __2-28-90__ , the student will demonstrate an increased competency in: GOAL — __division__ OBJ __Given 10 simple division prob. ex 2√12 or 6÷3 Jane will demonstrate she understands the concept by illustrating and finding the answers__	__Rap.__	__''*__	$\begin{array}{r}6\\2\overline{)12}\end{array}$ ⦿⦿⦿ ⦿⦿⦿	Achieved _____ Not Achieved _____ **METHODS OF MEASUREMENT** ☐ Observer ▣ Teacher Made Test ☐ Standardized Test ☐ CR Test ☐ Other __80% acc__
By __2-28-90__ , the student will demonstrate an increased competency in: GOAL — __family of facts__ OBJ __Jane will demonstrate she understands the interrelationship of x/÷ by writing a family of facts (5 prob 100% acc)__	__Rap.__	__**__	__ex.__ $2 \times 6 = 12$ $6 \times 2 = 12$ $12 \div 6 = 2$ $12 \div 2 = 6$	Achieved _____ Not Achieved _____ **METHODS OF MEASUREMENT** ☐ Observer ▣ Teacher Made Test ☐ Standardized Test ☐ CR Test ☐ Other
By __2-28-90__ , the student will demonstrate an increased competency in: GOAL — __story prob__ OBJ __Jane will write 2 each +,-,x,÷ story problems correctly expressed and show the correct ans to each__	__Rap.__			Achieved _____ Not Achieved _____ **METHODS OF MEASUREMENT** ☐ Observer ☐ Teacher Made Test ☐ Standardized Test ☐ CR Test ▣ Other __Sample__
By __2-28-90__ , the student will demonstrate an increased competency in: GOAL — __Voc. dev.__ OBJ __Given 25 words Jane will write a correct antonym for each (correctly spelled)__	__Rap.__	__**__		Achieved _____ Not Achieved _____ **METHODS OF MEASUREMENT** ☐ Observer ▣ Teacher Made Test ☐ Standardized Test ☐ CR Test ☐ Other

SE-51 (Rev. 7/87)   This is not a contract for services   White — Program Supervisor or District Office   Canary — Teacher   Pink — Parent   Goldenrod — Cum File   Circle all revisions of IEP with date and parent, teacher and administrator's initials

Diff Standard 75%

15 goals x 75% = 12 goals will be achieved

137

Sample Lesson

Lesson: Language development

Goal: Given a list of twenty-five words, students will write an antonym for each. Remind students that the lesson will prepare them to meet an IEP goal (raise their level of concern).

Give each child a pretest.

up _____	early _____
in _____	hard _____
first _____	day _____
short _____	start _____
big _____	good _____
go _____	sweet _____
hot _____	north _____
fast _____	east _____
black _____	can _____
old _____	to _____
boy _____	fat _____
dark _____	open _____
happy _____	

Answers: down, out, last, tall, little/small, come, cold, slow, white, young, girl, light, sad, late, soft, night, stop, bad, sour, south, west, can't, from, thin, shut (must be spelled correctly).

Help each child make a graph, and record their starting score.

Input: Give each child a completed ditto with answers to take home (have extras in case they lose theirs).

Daily practice: Give out a ditto. (They are to complete it in pen or crayon.) Go over answers orally at the end of each session (use overhead). If they say they know it, test them under test conditions with a fresh ditto.

As you do this lesson daily and students see their score moving higher, the lesson becomes intrinsically motivating. As slower students see others becoming "helpers," they become motivated not to be the last to learn it.

Number of antonyms known

Day 1		Day 2
25		25
24		24
23		23
22		22
21		21
20		20
19		19
18		18
17		17
16		16
15		15
14		14
13		13
12		12
11		11
10		10
9		9
8		8
7		7
6		6
5		5
4		4
3		3
2		2
1		1

The students will draw a bar to the correct height to represent the number they got right each day.

Day 1   Day 2   Day 3   and so on

Explain that they will be trying to beat their own score—not each other.

Tell them that on the day they get 100%, they can

1. become "helpers" of others,
2. get their IEP goal checked off,
3. choose a prize, and
4. take their progress graphs home.

SAMPLE LESSON (WITH CRUTCH)

Have the child give you a sentence orally, finding the needed words in the key below. Have the child repeat the sentence, then write it from memory.

1. _____

_____

2. _____

_____

3. _____

_____

4. _____

_____

Two	desk	are going	on
These	children	are playing	for
The	girls	are jumping	into
A	books		around
	game		
	swim		
	pool		
	water		

TEACHING SPELLING SKILLS TO LD STUDENTS

Spelling and writing skills go hand in hand with reading. When a child shows that he can blend two or three letters to make words (reading), you will want to teach him to unblend (spelling). For example, you say a word such as *not* and he listens for each sound *n o t*. Have him write words either on the chalkboard or on paper as he unblends them.

The ability to unblend is critical to becoming a decent speller. At first you may have to exaggerate the individual sounds. As you go on, however, the student will need to learn how to say the word (to say it again slower and slower until he can hear each sound). For initial practice, use only words where every letter is audible, and tell him how many sounds he should be looking for.

Here is a list that can be used to teach the beginning spelling skill of unblending:

at	cap	bus	rob	slam	fast
up	cup	drum	ran	grab	just
am	cut	cram	long	wag	snug
us	bag	last	must	hot	put
on	rag	lamp	jump	hop	pad
in	rug	nut	trap	drop	snap
if	rust	but	dot	fun	top

There are many other techniques that you can employ to help students learn to spell words. I will briefly discuss the following:

1. Configuration
2. Scramble and unscramble
3. Missing letter
4. Color-coding
5. Clay-spelling
6. Dot-to-dot
7. Writing with resistance
8. Manipulative letters
9. Word searches and puzzles
10. Proofreading
11. Syllabication and structural analysis
12. Teacher-guided practice using rhythm and pitch
13. Master list crutch
14. Memory tricks and patterns

Configuration. In configuration, the student has a list of words. You need to go over that list with each student until he can demonstrate that he can say every word. Then he matches the word to its configuration on a worksheet such as this:

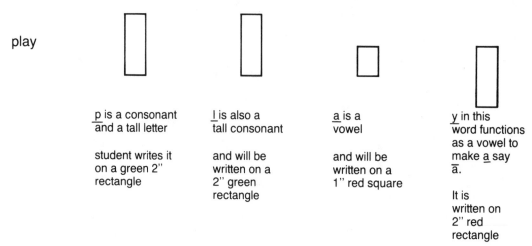

she		becomes	i s
not			(the)
is			(she)
here			(to)
come			(here)
can			(not)
play			(come)
to			(can)
the			(play)

On a second day, you can present the student with pieces of red and green paper. (For this lesson, you will need eleven red 1 inch squares and one 2 inch red rectangle and eight green 1 inch squares plus eight green 2 inch rectangles.) The student will select enough pieces of the correct size and color to form the word that he is trying to learn, paste them on a paper, then write the letters on the squares:

play

p is a consonant and a tall letter

student writes it on a green 2" rectangle

l is also a tall consonant

and will be written on a 2" green rectangle

a is a vowel

and will be written on a 1" red square

y in this word functions as a vowel to make a say a.

It is written on 2" red rectangle

Scramble and unscramble. Looking at his word list and a list of jumbled words, he matches them by drawing a line, thus:

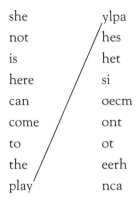

she	ylpa
not	hes
is	het
here	si
can	oecm
come	ont
to	ot
the	eerh
play	nca

On the third day, the student can be given an envelope containing red and green letters. First he separates them into vowels and consonants, then he selects the correct letters to spell each word.

Students can be taught to make a scramble list for a friend to decode.

Missing letter. The student has his word list. He must supply the missing letter or letters in his spelling words:

__ h e	p__ a y	__ __ m e
s h __	__ __ a y	c __ m __
s __ e	p l __ __	c o m __

Children can also be taught to make activities such as this for a friend to do. As they construct activities for a friend, their attention to detail is focused.

Color-coding. In previous activities, I have mentioned using red for vowels, green for consonants. Students can write their spelling words with crayons one day, water paint another, red and green pens or pencils the next.

Clay-spelling. Using modeling clay (sometimes called *Plasticene*) in red and green, the student rolls out ropes of clay and forms the words with clay. This activity is very effective. It requires them to think about each letter.

Dot-to-dot. This is also a highly effective technique. Students are told to write their spelling list dot-to-dot, for example:

Then they exchange papers and trace over what a friend has written in the dot-to-dot. (This is important because the friend will let them know if it's not clear.)

At first some students will say that they can't do this, but they catch on quickly.

Writing with resistance. Using the clay, students roll out a big flat square. Next they write their spelling list into clay using a stylus (pencil).

Manipulative letters. Felt squares with letters written on them, or tiles (1 inch ceramic tile) with letters written on them, can be arranged to form a word.

Word searches and puzzles. It is easy to make your own word searches. Begin by putting down the words you want on the graph paper:

						s	h	e								
	n	o	t								p	l	a	y		
					i	s			t	o						
					c	a	n				h	e	l	p		
	c	o	m	e												
					h	e	r	e								

Next you simply go back and add letters to the empty spaces.
Simple beginning crosswords might look like this:

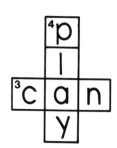

Across

1. _____ can play.

3. Tom _____ help mom.

Down

2. _____ cat sat on a mat.

4. She is in the _____ .

Proofreading. Proofreading can be enjoyable. (Proofreading also makes a good homework activity.) It does not really work well until the student is reading at a reading level of about 2.0 and can decode words well. Here is a sample lesson:

Dear Tom,

I *waz* glad to get *yer not.* We had a *goob tim* at your *horse.* I *lik* that game we *plaid.* I *well* show *yoo* a new game next time I *cee* you. *Mi* mom and *did sayd* we will *com* to see you *agin* in *Mae.*

Wish *luv,*
Sue

The misspelled words should be words that the student has had either in this lesson or in a previous one. This is a great way to do review. The student rewrites the paragraph, correcting all errors. Give some sort of tangible reward if he finds all the errors. Make it a game.

Syllabication and structural analysis. These are wonderful skills that can do marvelous things for students. A beginning reader encounters only one-syllable words, but by the time the student reaches grade 2 reading, he can learn wonderful things by doing this activity. For example:

before	*becomes*	bē fŏr
enough		ē nuf
remember		rē mem br
proud		prowd
strange		strānj
bicycle		bī sī kl
truck		truk
write		rīt

You are asking students to write what they hear. At this point, they do not use a dictionary. You help them listen for what is heard instead of how the word is actually spelled. They will pick up subtleties, such as that in *w r* words the *w* is silent. Now they can check their listening by using a dictionary. This activity can become a game if they are encouraged to compete against themselves and to keep score.

Teacher-guided practice using rhythm and pitch. In teacher-guided practice, the student copies a word.

Step 1. Look at it together, say things like, "What are the first two letters?" "What is the last letter?" "What letter is in third position?"

Step 2. "Let's say it—unblend it. Which letters are silent?"

Step 3. "Now let's spell it aloud, looking at it." (Do this three or four times.)

Step 4. "Close your eyes and spell it." If they can't, go back and redo steps 1, 2, 3, and 4.

Step 5. "Close your eyes. Put your fingers in your ears. Spell it three times." (The purpose of closing the eyes is to eliminate visually distracting stimuli. The purpose of closing the ears is to eliminate auditory competing stimuli. The student's attention is then focused inward on the activity he's doing.)

Step 6. "Write the word in the air with your finger."

Step 7. "Write it again on paper." With some words, you may want to add some rhythm to assist. For example, patting the hand on *first* would go

```
        f           ir          st
        .           ..          ..
   1 pat       2 quick     2 quick
                  pats        pats
```

Word and *help* are words often misspelled. Rhythm can straighten them out: The student says the letters as he taps the table

```
   he              lp              wo      rk
   ..              ..              likewise
2 quick   (pause)   2 quick
   pats              pats
```

Pitch can be utilized. For instance, the student says,

"do [low pitch] es [high pitch] spells *does.*"

Master list crutch. Following is a list of high-frequency words. I have these words printed up on heavy blue paper. Each student gets three laminated copies—one to keep at home, one for his desk at school, and one to use in my room.

When in doubt about the spelling of the word, the student can look it up by first and last sounds. If the student wants to use a word not on this list, write the desired word on the student's card so that he can find the words he uses to express himself (this procedure individualizes the list).

Memory tricks and patterns. Many students have trouble with words such as *jeep.* They don't know whether it's *jepe, jeap,* or *jeep.* I often tell them to use a trick. If it's *jeep*—they exaggerate the *ee* sound by shaking their head as they study it. If it's the *ea* pattern, they touch their mouth (where they eat) when they are studying it while visualizing that they have an apple in their hand (*a*-apple).

When it's words like *mail* or *tray*—if it's an *i,* they touch their "eye." If it's *ay,* they study it as *tray—play*—saying, "tray/play" several times to remind themselves that the ending is the same.

TEACHING WRITING SKILLS TO LD STUDENTS

Many LD students have difficulty with written expression. Like other skills, improvement comes with practice. The more writing a student does, the more likely he is to become a competent speller and writer. Allowing students to use a spelling crutch (a word list) makes the task less frustrating, more pleasant.

When a child's reading skills reach second grade level, we want to teach him about forming correct sentences. You may do this by playing a game. The students are told that they are two-year olds again. They are to express themselves. I begin by pointing and saying, "I want."

MASTER WORD LIST

about	each	keep	ran	under
after	early	kind	read	until
again	eat	know	red	up
all	eight		ride	upon
also	end	last	run	us
always	every	laugh		use
am	eyes	leave	said	
an		left	same	very
and	face	let	sat	
any	fall	letter	saw	walk
are	far	light	say	want
around	fast	like	school	warm
as	fat	little	second	was
ask	find	live	see	wash
at	fine	long	seem	water
ate	fire	look	send	way
away	first	love	sent	we
	five		set	well
back	fly	made	seven	went
ball	food	make	shall	were
be	for	man	she	what
because	found	many	should	when
bed	four (4)	may	show	where
been	friend	me	sing	which
best	from	men	sister	while
better	full	might	sit	white
big	funny	money	six	who
black		more	sleep	why
blue	gave	morning	small	will
book	get	most	so	wish
both	girl	mother	some	with
box	give	much	soon	woman
boy	go	must	stand	work
bring	goes	my	start	would
brought	going	myself	stop	write
brown	good		such	
but	got	name	sure	year
buy	green	near		yesterday
	grow	never	take	you
call		new	taught	your
came	had	next	ten	
can	hand	night	than	_____'s words
car	happy	no	thank	
carry	hard	not	that	
cat	has	now	the	
clean	hat		their	
close	have	of	them	
clothes	he	off	then	
coat	head	old	there	
color	hear	on	these	

come	help	once	they
could	her	one	thing
cut	here	open	think
	high	or	third
day	him	other	this
dear	his	our	those
did	hold	out	thought
different	home	over	three
do	hope	own	through
does	hot		to
dog	house	pair	today
done	how	part	together
don't	hurt	people	too
door		pick	took
down	if	place	town
draw	in	play	tree
dress	is	please	try
drink	it	present	turn
		pretty	two (2)
	jump	pull	
	just	put	

Depending on the ability of the group, you may need to model further:

"Daddy go."

"Mama eat."

These are your simplest sentences—noun, verb. We discuss that nouns name people, places, or things. We make charts of nouns to hang. Then we hang a chart of helping verbs, a chart of action verbs, and a chart of phrases. The charts look like this:

Nouns	Helping Verbs	Action Verbs	Phrases
(people, places, things)	am will	run went	to the store
Dad	are was	sing drew	a gift
I Sally	can were	eat made	for my dad's birthday
you Mamma	did	like saw	a lot of smoke
he cat	do	find put	a letter in the mailbox
she tree	has	open help	us a ride
it office	had	look gave	us clean the house
we chair	have	came made	me a dollar
they water	is	work	up her mind slowly

Students are then asked to take these very simple sentences (noun, verb) and add a phrase. The chalkboard might look like this:

	us a ride (Tom)
Dad gave	me a dollar (Ann)
	him a spanking (David)
	me a haircut (Bill)
	us clean the house (Tom)
Mama made	a birthday cake for Dad (Ann)
	a picture of us (David)
	up her mind slowly (Bill)

It is possible to make up similar matching games. First, cut index cards into strips 3/4" × 2" long. Write nouns on several—*we, he, she, they, you, I, Dad, Mom, my, sister, Grandma*, or name objects such as

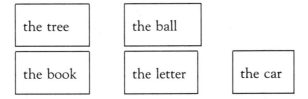

On the back, write the word *noun*. On other cards, write some verbs—*am, are, can, is, have, has, had, could, may, was, were, will, help, wrote, drive, visit, eating, read, hit, saw, do, gave*. Write the word *verb* on the back of each card.

On other cards, write phrases such as:

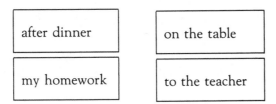

Two possible sentences a child could construct might be:

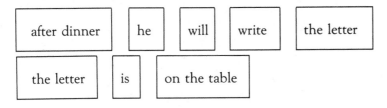

Using other choices, we might have

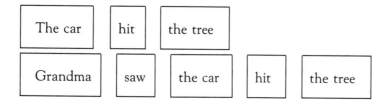

Put the word cards into an envelope. When the child gets the envelope, he sorts them, as follows:

nouns   verbs   noun phrases

Then he constructs sentences that he thinks make sense. He gets your approval. If it is correct, he writes it on paper, capitalizing the first word of the sentence and putting a period or question mark at the end of the sentence.

After several lessons on nouns, verbs, and phrases, most children begin to write very good sentences of their own without crutches. You can encourage them by reading to the whole class especially good sentences and saying, "Good. I like the phrase you added. That's what I like to see."

In grades 1 and 2, have students dictate short stories to you or to another adult who writes them down using proper mechanics and grammar. Then the student reads his story to two or three other students who take notes. Notes are a list of as many nouns and verbs as they can write down while listening.

In grade 3, you will want to begin paragraph writing. Many students have no idea what a paragraph is, so you have to show them. (Refer to the end of Chapter 3 for information regarding teaching about paragraphing.)

Rewriting familiar stories, such as "The Three Little Pigs," can help reluctant students begin to write. They write the story from memory in their own words.

Movies are a great way to provide the input necessary for a good writing lesson. "Which character did you identify with most?" "How are you like that person?" "Do you feel that he did what he should?" "Why?"

A process movie (for example, *How Raisins Are Made; How Paper Is Made*) can lead into writing how to do or make something. Process writing is important writing. It helps students clarify their thoughts, watch for sequence, and become better readers of directions.

If you know you will have at least three hours a week to devote to writing activities, the following project is a winner.

Students are divided into groups of four and you give them input on their writing assignment. They are told that they can get ideas or help from others in their group. When they finish what they are writing, it must be read for meaning by all members of their group. If it is not clear, the others in the group should say so and help the person change it so that it makes sense. Then these paragraphs are switched with another group. The second group reads them and selects the one that they consider best, but they must be prepared to justify why that one is best. Next the best offerings are read aloud and posted. Finally the teacher chooses a common need to discuss each week to improve their writing—at the beginning, it may be that the pronoun *I* must always be capitalized. Later it may be how to use quotation marks and how to punctuate conversation (for example, each time a new speaker speaks, you must indent). Another week it might be finding interesting ways to catch the reader's attention.

Once the lesson has been given, the students begin to look at their writing and the writing of others with that lesson in mind.

From this project students become much better writers and good editors. You may want to make a class notebook or newspaper to save their best efforts.

Clustering and brainstorming is another technique that is very effective in helping reluctant writers. The teacher supplies a main idea sentence such as

> Halloween is
> an exciting holiday.

The students are encouraged to add ideas in the form of key words, thus:

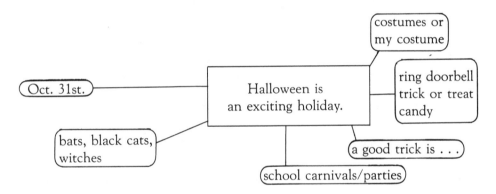

After all the ideas are listed on the chalkboard, the child selects a few to make into sentences for his paragraph or story.

Similarly, teachers can provide a stimulus picture with suggestive vocabulary.

Vocabulary box:

ghost	jack-o'-lantern
goblin	carve
broom	field
Halloween	haunted
dark	squeak
haystack	trick or treat
cobweb	skeleton
pumpkin	

Likewise, story starters are helpful. The best story starters relate to common child experiences such as:

Lost (child describes a time that he thought he was lost.)

Mom's/Dad's Mad

The New Baby

Home Alone at Night

Being Sick

Here is a sample story starter:

Directions: "Finish this story so that I know what happened to the puppy. Write a title for the story."

Tom was walking home from school. He was upset. He had not made a 100% on his spelling test, and that made him feel bad. His head was down, and he was deep in thought.

All at once he saw a small brown puppy under the bush. It was making soft crying sounds. Tom forgot the spelling and went to the puppy.

"Oh, you poor thing. Where is your mother?" He looked around, but no big dog could be seen.

The puppy leaned closer to Tom and began licking his hand. It seemed to say, "Take me home. Please don't leave me here."

"Oh, puppy. I'd like to take you with me, but I know my mom won't let me keep you."

_____

_____

_____

_____

_____

_____

If the student needs additional room, add more space or use an extra sheet of paper.

Suggested Topics for Student Writing

Elementary

The Ostrich (or any other interesting animal, such as a sloth, an aardvark, a fiddler crab)

My Favorite Dinosaur

The Color Red

How Ice Cream Cones Began

SAMPLE LESSON—SENTENCE WRITING

SAMPLE LESSON—PARAGRAPH WRITING

_____

_____

_____

_____

_____

_____

_____

_____

How Animals Protect Themselves

The Meaning of Traffic Signals

How to Grow Strong Bones and Teeth

What to Do in an Earthquake (or a hurricane or tornado)

How Glass Is Made

How Eskimos Live (or Indians)

Celebrating the New Year (or Christmas)

Parts of a Flower

What Is Magic?

How Light and Sound Travel

The Many Uses of Milk

Secondary

The Amazing Galapagos Islands

The Safest Colors for Cars

To Sleep—Perchance to Dream

How the Jeep Got Its Name

Diamonds

The Helpful Sneeze

Religions of the World (or a specific religion)

Music

Famous Sayings and What They Mean

POINTERS FOR HELPING THE LD CHILD IN MATH

Most children enjoy math, but about one in seven will experience difficulty in learning math. Sometimes the problem is due to poor learning; other times the child is dyscalculic. Just as dyslexia covers a wide array of specific deficits, so does this term.

I would need several books to write everything about the teaching of math. In the limited space here, I'll make suggestions about commonly seen deficits and ways to help.

Skill: Counting and one-to-one correspondence.   For a student to become good at math, it is essential that he be able to count accurately.

For a beginning student, the amounts 0 to 10 are taught. He needs to use manipulatives—one day, beans; the next, blocks; the next, crayons; and so forth. Some teachers teach the song, "One Little, Two Little, Three Little Indians." They are tapping into the right-brain hemisphere to support the child's memory—a helpful technique. Once the child counts 0 to 10, he needs to be able to count sets. Begin with sets that have 0 to 3 objects.

The child uses his finger to touch each member of the set, saying a number each time he touches a new object. (Moving the object helps.)

When he is proficient, you can add 4, 5, 6. When those one-to-one correspondences are established, you can add 7, 8, 9, 10.

Next you will want to teach him to add; use sets totaling 10 or less. Teach the child to put the larger number in his head and the smaller number on his fingers—4 + 2, four goes into his head and he holds up two fingers. Tapping his head, he says *one, two, three, four,* and then he touches each finger for *five, six.* As time goes on, he will not have to tap *one, two, three, four,* but can just begin at *four.*

Once addition facts 0 to 10 are taught, teach him the matching subtraction facts.

He needs to learn about families of facts, as follows:

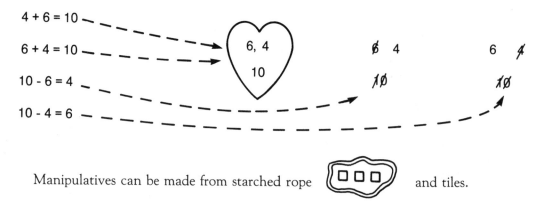

Manipulatives can be made from starched rope and tiles.

When the student is comfortable with facts 0 to 10 and has them firmly in his memory, teach him to count on to 18. Next he will be able to complete learning his addition and subtraction facts to 18.

The next counting task is 0 to 100. If the student is young, teach him by using the method shown in this chapter.

For the older student just coming into special education services, test for the following understandings:

1. Ask the student to count from 0 to 100.

2. On flash cards, write several numbers—28, 42, 71. Present these randomly and see if he can call them correctly. If he says *82* for *28,* he has a sequencing problem.

3. Present him with a stack of 20 small cubes 1″ × 1″ and let him look at them for 10 seconds. Cover them and ask him to make a guess as to how many there are. Any answer from 15 to 25 is acceptable.

If he cannot do any of these tasks, you probably need to start by teaching him to count orally from 0 to 100, to write the numbers both serially and randomly, and to approximate how many (using cubes, beans, poker chips, or blocks). The ditto that follows will help.

Once the student can count and write to 100 by himself (he does a ditto daily until

	0	**1**	**2**	**3**	**4**	**5**	**6**	**7**	**8**	**9**
The child learns to start everything on this line with 1	10	11	1	1	1					
everything here begins with 2; he calls the 2 "twenty"										
he calls the "thirty" 3										
"forty" 4										
"fifty" 5										
"sixty" 6										
"seventy" 7										
"eighty" 8										
"ninety" 9										
10	100									

As the student writes *two,* you say *twenty.* As he brings down the 3, you say "three." He needs to write quickly enough to be hearing "twenty-three" not "twenty . . . three."

he can do it correctly on his own without prompting), then you need to point to random numbers until he can say them without hesitating.

Another counting activity that can be taught here if you wish, or slightly later, is rote memory of the 2's: 0, 2, 4, 6, 8, 10, 12, 14, 16, 18—and the 5's table to 100.

When the student is ready to learn to add 47 + 5, he just says, "47 in my head and 5 on my fingers" and counts as he did for easy addition problems.

Skill: *Understanding the more/less concept.* Using manipulatives, teach the child to look and say, "9 is more than 5 and 5 is less than 9."

Some children do this skill fine but are confused when asked to use the symbols < and >. This is easy to straighten out. Put the problem down 9 ○ 5. Say, "Which is more?" If the child says 9, have him place 2 dots by the nine and 1 dot by the 5—for example, 9 ☺ 5. By connecting the dots, he has the correct symbol >.

Skill: *Place value is a critical concept.* It is best taught by buying craft sticks and putting them in groups of 10 (rubber band) 100 (larger rubber band). The student needs to learn to read numbers and to understand what it means.

$$\frac{\overparen{3 \quad\quad 6 \quad\quad 4}}{100 \quad 10 \quad 1} \quad \text{Column}$$

The student puts out 3 sets of 100, 6 sets of 10, and 4 individual sticks. They must understand that 3 hundred is 100

$$\begin{array}{r} 100 \\ 100 \\ \underline{100} \\ 300 \end{array} \quad \text{and}$$

6 tens is 10 + 10 + 10 + 10 + 10 + 10 = 60

4 ones is 1 + 1 + 1 + 1 = 4.

$$\begin{array}{r} 300 \\ 60 \\ \underline{4} \\ 364 \end{array}$$

Skill: *Addition and subtraction with regrouping.* When you begin to teach two-digit addition, for example

$$\begin{array}{r} 3|5 \\ + 1|5 \\ \hline 0 \end{array}$$

you may want to get out the craft sticks again for a few days so that he understands about putting a rubber band around 5 + 5 = 10 and adding that 1 to the tens place. When adding

$$\begin{array}{r} 3|0 \\ + 2|7 \end{array}$$

the students must learn to say, "I have none [not zero] over here and 7 over there. How much is that in all?"

The reason students do not learn to subtract is that they do not know how to talk a problem through. You cannot learn to do subtraction without this conversation (out loud at first; later you can talk it through in your head). I believe that it is critical to mix problems requiring regrouping and not requiring regrouping from the beginning. Teach students to talk out what they are doing. Tell them, "The number on top is what you have"; for example,

Students must talk each problem out step by step.

I have "none." Can I take away 7? No. I go next door and say *can you loan me one?* He has 3 left. I put the 1 in front of the zero. Now I have 10. Can I take away 7? Yes. I have 3. Can I take away one? Yes. I have 2 left.

$$
\begin{array}{r} 40 \\ -\ 17 \end{array}
$$

$$3\,40$$

$$
\begin{array}{r} 3\,410 \\ -\ 1\ 7 \\ \hline 2\ 3 \end{array}
$$

When he encounters a problem such as
$$
\begin{array}{r} 601 \\ -\ 289 \end{array}
$$
it works the same.

These are the words to teach students to say.

The student says I have one. Can I take away 9?" No. I go next door to borrow one. The neighbor says, I have none, sorry. So I go 2 houses down. Can I borrow 1? Yes. He now has 5. I take it next door. Now I have 10. Can I borrow one now? Yes. That leaves 9. I now have 11. Can I subtract 9? Yes. I have 9. Can I subtract 8? Yes. I have 5. Can I subtract 2? Yes.

$$
\begin{array}{r} 601 \\ -\ 289 \end{array}
$$

$$5\,6\ 0\ 1$$

$$5\,6\ 10\ 1$$

$$
\begin{array}{r} 5\quad\ 9 \\ 6\quad 10\ 11 \\ -\ 2\quad\ 8\quad 9 \\ \hline \end{array}
$$

When you first begin this, it is far better for a student to do 3 problems a day right (with you watching each step and helping him talk it through) than to learn it all wrong and have to unlearn and relearn it.

As students can add and subtract, you need to begin to teach them to read and to do simple word problems.

In addition, we put things together (join them):

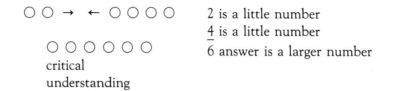

○ ○ → ← ○ ○ ○ ○   2 is a little number
                                  4 is a little number
○ ○ ○ ○ ○   6 answer is a larger number
critical
understanding

Example of a simple word problem:

I have five fish. I get three more fish. How many fish do I have now?

Teach the child to write 8 *fish*, not just 8.

In subtraction, we start with a larger number and end up with a smaller number. For example,

$$\begin{array}{r} 18 \\ -\ 9 \\ \hline 9 \end{array}$$

In beginning word problems, students need to draw pictures to go with the problems you write. In the addition example, the child draws five ⋈ and three ⋈ and counts. For example, ⋈ ⋈ ⋈ ⋈ ⋈ + ⋈ ⋈ ⋈

They also need to learn to write their own word problem. They often like to use the names of their classmates. Writing simple problems sharpens their spelling skills.

Skill: Reading number words. Once students are working in the hundreds column, you want to teach them to spell number words and to convert number words to digits.

Put the following on a ditto or a copying machine.

one	=	1	eleven	=	11	thirty	=	30
two	=	2	twelve	=	12	forty	=	40
three	=	3	thir*teen*	=	13	fifty	=	50
four	=	4	four*teen*	=	14	sixty	=	60
five	=	5	fif*teen*	=	15	seventy	=	70
six	=	6	six*teen*	=	16	eighty	=	80
seven	=	7	seven*teen*	=	17	ninety	=	90
eight	=	8	eigh*teen*	=	18			
nine	=	9	nine*teen*	=	19	hundred	=	100
ten	=	10	twenty	=	20			

Grade Two—Sample Lesson (using the chart)

Write the number for

thirty-five   __ __ __

six hundred, forty-one   __ __ __

one hundred and five   __ __ __

Note: This last problem requires that students understand that there is a zero in the tens column.

Write the number words for

    a. 410 _____

    b.   73 _____

    c. 129 _____

In later grades, use the same sort of lessons. At grade 3, add the thousands column:

<table>
<tr><td>

____ ____ ____ ____
   | | | ones
   | | tens
   | hundreds
thousands

</td><td>

1. Students need to read numbers.

2. They need to write numbers if the number words are given and to do the reverse process of changing numbers into words and writing them.

Later the ten thousands, hundred thousands, and millions columns are added.

</td></tr>
</table>

Skill: Multiplication and division.   Multiplication and division should be taught together as you did with addition and subtraction.

When the child is presented with 3×4, he is taught to draw three groups. Next he places four marks in each group. .... He counts marks: $3 \times 4 = 12$. Point out the similarity to adding; 3×4 is the same as $4 + 4 + 4$ (joining). 3×4 means "three fours."

He needs to make a family of facts:

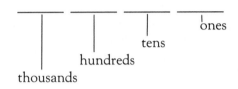

$3 \times 4 = 12$

$4 \times 3 = 12$

$12 \div 4 = 3$ .... becomes

$12 \div 3 = 4$ ...   . becomes

Division, like subtraction, is removing groups from the whole:

$$
\begin{array}{r}
12 \\
- \;\;③ \\
\hline
9 \\
- \;\;③ \\
\hline
6 \\
- \;\;③ \\
\hline
3 \\
- \;\;③ \\
\hline
0
\end{array}
$$

    four 3's can be removed.

He needs to recognize that $3\overline{)12}$ is the same as $12 \div 3$. Next show him how to handle subscript numbers, as in

$$4\overline{)9} \quad \begin{array}{r} 2\ r\ 1 \\ \hline \end{array}$$

and show remainder.

$$\begin{array}{r} -\ 8 \\ \hline 1 \end{array}$$

He must learn to read his answer. "I have 2 groups of 4 and there is 1 left over."

He needs to do multiplication and division story problems and to write his own story problems.

I have found the matrix to be one of the handiest ways to teach multiplication and division facts.

For example, on the 2's horizontally the student says $2 + 2 = 4$. He writes 4, then he says, $4 + 2 = 6$, and so on.

By having students repeat 2, 4, 6, 8 10 orally daily, their auditory memory is triggered. Once the 2's table is learned, do the 3's table daily until it's learned.

By asking students, "What numbers never appear?" they see that certain numbers, for example, 11, 13, 19 . . . 53, cannot be factored.

Using the matrix like a grid, they can locate 3×6 (down 3, across 6 is 18) or $6\overline{)18}$ (down 6, across to 18), look at top for other member of this family of facts. Allowing them to make and use their matrix daily will facilitate the memorization of the times tables.

When you're ready to teach the child to multiply 2 digits by 1, do this:

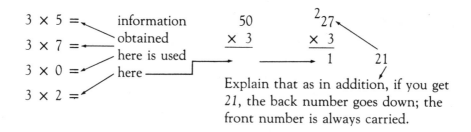

Explain that as in addition, if you get *21*, the back number goes down; the front number is always carried.

When students are learning to multiply $\begin{array}{r} 35 \\ \times\ 64 \\ \hline \end{array}$ the student must understand that there are two simpler problems here:

$$\begin{array}{r} 35 \\ \times\ \ 4 \\ \hline 140 \end{array} \qquad \text{and} \qquad \begin{array}{r} 35 \\ \times\ \ 6 \\ \hline 210. \end{array}$$

Then he simply combines them by using a space holder.

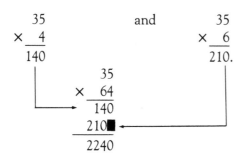

MATRIX

X	1	2	3	4	5	6	7	8	9	10
1	1	2	3	4	5	6	7	8	9	10
2	2									
3	3									
4	4									
5	5									
6	6									
7	7									
8	8									
9	9									
10	10									

When teaching long division, start with problems you can illustrate, such as:

$2\overline{)90}$ Draw 90 marks on their ditto

Teach steps

÷ (answer goes on top)

×

—

b.d. (stands for bring down)

. . . .
. . . .
. . . .
. . . .
. . . .
. . . .
. . . .
. . . .
. . . .

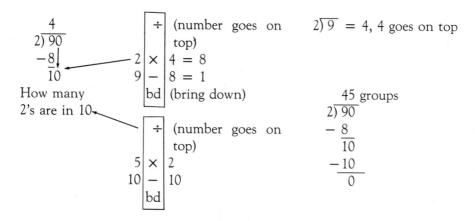

When you get an answer of 45 groups, go back to the lines and have the students prove it by circling every two marks and counting the groups they make.

Move on to teaching steps

Teach students to check their answer by using multiplication 45 × 2 = 90. When they read their answer, be sure that they say 45 *groups* of 2, instead of just 45. When you are ready to begin two-digit division,

15)60   The LD student must ex-   ⓁⓈ   30
          periment until he has some   ⓁⓈ
          concept of what would be   15 = 45
          a reasonable guess.   15 = 60

Most arithmetic texts do not provide adequate practice on this skill, so you will need to supplement this practice. It is a mistake to go on to the next skill until the student can guess how many 16's are in 93, or how many 24's are in 78, and so on.

Skill: Telling time.   Teaching students to tell time was once a critical skill. Now, with digital watches, it is not as important as it once was. If you are going to teach it, there are some basic concepts that must first be taught:

1.   How to count by 5's (to 60)

2.   How to tell what hour it is. (It is critical for the student to realize that both hands are moving clockwise and that the minute hand moves faster than the hour hand.)

3.   The student must know (beyond a shadow of a doubt) that the shorter hand is the hour hand.

Several lessons should be presented where the student is asked only: "What hour is it?"

  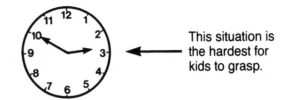

They say 3, but now you must have them watch both hands on large real clocks as they move simultaneously so that they grasp that it's not 3:00 until the minute hand is on the 12.

When this is clear—absolutely understood—then you will be able to teach them to count the minutes *after* an hour or minutes until the next hour.

Later you will want to give problems such as:

It's 3:10 now. What time will it be in 20 more minutes?

You have to catch a bus at 4 o'clock, and it's 3:10 now. How many minutes must you wait?

Your plane leaves at 6:15. You need to know what time to start getting ready to leave. It takes you 30 minutes to dress, 20 minutes to drive to the airport, and you feel you should allow 30 minutes just in case something goes wrong. What time should you get up?

Skill: Money.   Money skills are essential skills for survival. With LD students, it is best to use real coins.

First they must recognize the coins—and understand their value.

The penny is "brown," worth 1¢.

The nickel is "silver," but it's not made of silver—it's made from nickel, so it's worth less than silver. It is worth 5¢.

The dime is "silver"—it is a small coin, worth 10¢.

The quarter is "silver"—it is a larger coin, worth 25¢.

The half-dollar is "silver," it is larger yet, worth 50¢.

They must understand equal amounts, 5 pennies is the same as a nickel, 2 nickels is the same as a dime, and so on. They need to count it—show you various amounts and other ways to make the same amount as you show them.

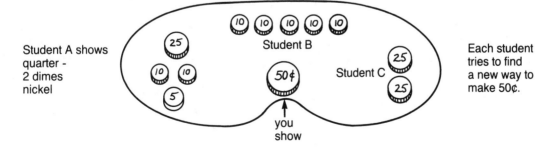

Student A shows
quarter -
2 dimes
nickel

Student B

Student C

you show

Each student tries to find a new way to make 50¢.

Use a chart to help students count money.

They should place coins on squares as they count (for example, put a quarter on a 25 square and count 10 forward leaving a dime on a 35 square, and so on).

The chart can also be used for helping a student make change for amounts under $1.00. He begins by placing a dot to represent a package. Once change is figured, have him pretend to be a clerk. He places a package in your hand, saying "69¢, 70¢ (as he adds a penny), 75¢ (as he adds the nickel), and $1.00" (as he adds the quarter). At first you will have to say the numbers, and he will have to repeat them. The student needs to realize that there are some numbers that are more important—numbers ending in 5 or 0; 25¢, 50¢, 75¢, and $1.00.

Skill: Understanding and using graphs, tables, and scales. The bar graph and pie graph are important to teach. The most efficient way to get students to remember the elements is to help them construct graphs on something that they are doing. The more relevant it is, the more they usually gain. For example:

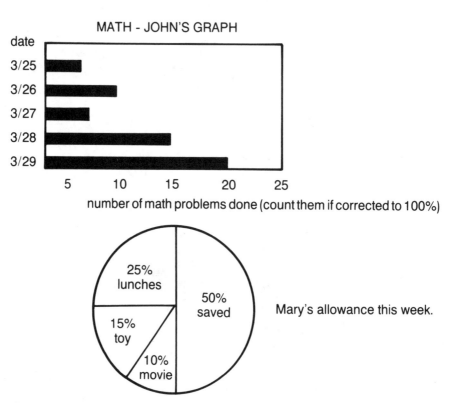

As tables and graphs come up in texts, encourage students to read them and explain them orally.

Scales are best taught with real scale experiences. As you gradually put something on the scale, they can see the arrow moving clockwise to a larger amount. A walking trip to a nearby supermarket can serve to teach many lessons if they are carefully planned. On

0	1	2	3	4	5	6	7	8	9
10	11	12	13	14	15	16	17	18	19
20	21	22	23	24	25	26	27	28	29
30	31	32	33	34	35	36	37	38	39
40	41	42	43	44	45	46	47	48	49
50	51	52	53	54	55	56	57	58	59
60	61	62	63	64	65	66	67	68	69
70	71	72	73	74	75	76	77	78	79
80	81	82	83	84	85	86	87	88	89
90	91	92	93	94	95	96	97	98	99
100									

the walk, have students construct a crude map of street names and major points of interest. The map can be refined and redrawn later.

In the supermarket, scale skills can be demonstrated. Allow students to practice weighing items.

Mathematically you can ask which is a better bargain—four bars of soap in a package for $1.67 or four bars bought separately? What is the savings? What is the per-unit price for the packaged bars? Allow children to watch as clerks make change.

Point out and check for use of classification skills. Where did you find syrup? Where are the apples kept? Where is the cheese? Store occupations can be a topic discussed prior to their trip. Let them interview various workers about what they do, how they like it, what they feel is important to know. Ask the children to point out to you some examples of the use of art in the store while you are there. Most stores are happy to have you come—especially during slower hours. As a post-trip experience, schedule evaluative activities: If you were to manage this store, how would you make it better?

Skill: Understanding fractions.

Fractions can be fun to teach. Here is a good way to introduce a fractions lesson: Tell students that you are going to let them have either 1/6 of a bar of candy or 1/3. Write their names on the board and ask them which they want. Put their fractional choice beside their names. Then get out the candy and divide large bars into 1/6 and 1/3 and distribute saying, "Here is your 1/6th" or "your 1/3rd." Immediately and graphically you have taught a lesson. One-third's are bigger than one-sixth's. It is a critical concept to understand—as the denominator (teach the term and what it means) gets larger, the piece gets smaller.

Making manipulatives:

Give each student 20 circles (8 inches in diameter).

Have them reserve 3 (wholes).

Have them fold all others in half.

Have them cut 3 into halves marking each side as

$$\frac{1 \text{ piece}}{2 \text{ pieces}} \xrightarrow{} (1 \text{ piece out of } 2 \text{ pieces})$$

Student must understand what this line means.

Taking 3 others, which have been folded in halves, fold them equally again, to make fourths.

They cut them into fourths, marking each piece 1/4 or 1 piece out of 4.

Likewise, do eighths by folding again. Mark each piece 1/8.

Take the remaining halves, help the students to fold the remaining 3 circles so that they have sixths. (Mark each piece *1/6*.)

Students keep their pieces (put their initials on the back of each piece) in an envelope for future use.

Ask students to compare sizes of pieces. Example: Which is more? Less?

$$< \quad >$$

| 1/4 | ○ | 1/8 | 1/4 | ○ | 1/2 |
| 1/6 | ○ | 1/3 | 1/2 | ○ | 1/3 |

Second day: Repeat lesson with squares, not circles.

Using sheets of square paper, cut one in half (label parts), another into fourths, another into eighths, another into sixths, another into thirds. Halve the thirds again to make sixths.

Third day:

Objective: Teach them to say and spell the word *denominator* and explain its meaning. For example: Write 6/6. The child says "I had a whole [name a suitable object—such as pie, apple, cake]. I cut it into 6 pieces. If I have all 6 pieces, I still have all of it even though it's cut."

Write another fraction, 4/4, and continue to say the same sort of thing: "I had a cake. I cut it into 4 parts. As long as no one eats any, I have the whole cake."

Later, teach the word *numerator* and what it means: 3/4 means that "something was divided into 4 pieces, but I have only 3 pieces. If I had one more, I'd have all of it." Likewise, 4/7: "Something was divided into 7 pieces. I have 4. If I had 3 more, I'd have all of them." Students repeat.

Practice is needed until the child can independently, unerringly complete any problem by stating how many pieces are needed to make a whole.

$$3/4 + \square = 4/4 = 1 \quad 4/7 + \square = 7/7 = 1$$

Once students clearly understand what *numerator* and *denominator* mean, you should have them use their fractional pieces to look at problems such as 12/8 or 3/6 and tell you the equivalent amounts.

They sometimes need hundreds of manipulative experiences to understand the concept of more than 1, less than 1, and equivalent amounts.

If more than 1, they need to learn to state what it is the same as. For example: 12/8 is $1\frac{1}{2}$ (seen by placing parts together).

This more-than-1, less-than-1 must be mastered before going to the next step.

To teach LD students to reduce, tell them to divide both numerator and denominator—use 2, 3, 5, or 7. If none of these numbers work, the fraction probably can't be reduced; 8/12 becomes 4/6, which then becomes 2/3.

Students should not proceed until they thoroughly understand equivalent amounts. It is best to teach it in both directions.

$$2\,\overline{\smash{\big)}\,4/6} = 2/3 \qquad \frac{2}{3} \times \frac{2}{2} = \frac{4}{6} \times \frac{2}{2} = \frac{8}{12} \times \frac{2}{2} = \text{and so on}$$

Teach addition and subtraction of like fractions; for example, 3/4 + 3/4, 5/8 + 1/8. Teach addition and subtraction of mixed numbers, $1\frac{1}{2} + 2\frac{1}{2}$. (Have them confirm their answers with their fractional parts.)

$$O D + O O D = 4$$

Students who have understood the previous concepts are now ready for either adding or subtracting unlike fractions or moving on to multiplication and division of like fractions.

The ability to add, subtract, multiply, and divide fractions is not essential to most of our lives; however, we are called upon to use them in measuring. Students need a variety of experiences measuring, dealing with fractions—halves, thirds, fourths, sixths, and eighths.

Skill: Understanding and using measurement.

Students need to be proficient in the ability to measure. Men and women need to measure for curtains and to use linear measurement in home-building projects.

This can also be fun to teach. You will need several sets of teaspoons, tablespoons, funnels, and measuring cups. You will also need several cartons of each size—pint, quart, gallon.

Let them answer questions by the discovery method. Use water to experiment with and to learn answers to questions such as: How many cups are in a quart? How many ounces are in a cup? Cooking experiences at home and at school will increase their proficiency. To teach linear measurement, let students measure objects by the inch, foot, or yard.

Skill: Decimals and percents.

Students will need to be able to convert decimals to percents. This skill can be made relevant by having them figure their own grades. When you return papers showing the number right over the number possible (for example, 4/5), the child can learn to convert it to a percentage score $5\,\overline{\smash{\big)}\,4.0} = 80\%$.

Skill: Relating math experiences to life.

For LD students, who show deficits in math, we need to teach them the kind of math problems needed for everyday life—for example, in addition and subtraction, we need to teach students how to write checks (spell number words), keep a checkbook register, and reconcile an account. We need to teach students how to figure the kind of problems involving percentage used to figure sales tax, income tax, and social security forms. In division, they need to learn to calculate per-unit prices so that they can make comparisons at the store (you may bypass this by teaching the skill of looking for posted per-unit price at the market or using a calculator to figure the per-unit cost).

Skill: Finding an average. This skill can also be related to student life. The students can be given their test scores

```
 100          3 ⌐260
  90        tests  points
  70
 ───
 260
```

and allowed to compute their average score. Teach them to transfer this skill to problems such as, "I used 9 gallons of gas to drive 270 miles. What was my average miles per gallon?" (If you have a student who has spatial deficits and finds it difficult to keep columns straight, larger-squared graph paper will be helpful.)

Math Story Problem Clues

Addition (putting sets together)	*Subtraction* (taking sets apart)
How many in all?	Find the difference.
How many all together?	How many more/less?
What is the sum?	How much bigger?
What is the total?	taller?
	(comparing
	2 numbers) heavier?
	older?
Multiplication (putting equal sets together)	*Division* (taking equal sets apart)
How many in all?	Find the average.
How many all together?	What would one unit be?
product	If shared
	divided
	Find the quotient.

TEACHING REFERENCE SKILLS

Do LD students need to learn reference skills? Several years ago, I was observing a junior high school special day class teacher, trying in vain to teach her students to use card catalog cards. The mood in the room was one of frustration. In discussing the lesson later, I asked her the reading level of her group. She told me that she had one nonreader and

SAMPLE DAILY WORKSHEET, GRADE 3

Review Skills

63	79	80	45	72
+28	+43	+16	+25	+28

63	79	80	45	72
−28	−43	−16	−25	−28

Newer Skills

$3 \times 5 =$ 305 $3 \times 7 =$ 247
                    $\times\ \ 3$ $\times\ \ 3$

$3 \times 3 =$ $3 \times 2 =$

$3 \times 0 =$ $3 \times 4 =$

0, 3, 6, ____, 12, ____, ____, 21, ____, 27, ____

$3\overline{)\ 10}$ . . . . .

$3\overline{)\ 19}$ . . . . .
                    . . . . .
                    . . . . .
                    . . . .

Application Problems

a) Jane is nine. Sam is six. How much older is Jane? _____

b) You have a dozen cookies to share with me. How many will each of us get? _____

c) Three teams. Four kids on each team. There are _____ players.

Story Problems

d) Write a subtraction problem of your own.

e) Write a multiplication problem of your own.

f) Write a division problem of your own.

that her best reader's skills were about third grade. After further questioning, I learned that none of her students liked to read. When asked why she was trying to teach card catalog skills, she reported that she was expected to do so in eighth grade.

In this case, it was not appropriate. Even though she was a new teacher, she was finally able to talk courageously to her principal about her students' real needs—to learn to read, to learn to add, subtract, multiply, and divide, to learn to spell. From that point on, she weighed all curriculum expectancies for validity. Teacher judgment is a very important element in teaching.

Reference skills are needed by students who will go on to finish high school and possibly go on to college. These are students with mild to moderate learning disabilities, with IQ scores above 100, and who are only slightly behind their grade level expectancy.

Dictionary

The first dictionary a student uses is probably one that he will make. In third grade reading, students normally begin to encounter a few words with which they are not familiar. They usually make a loose-leaf dictionary with a page for words of each alphabet letter (no effort is made to alphabetize words by second, third, or other letters). It is wise at this point to teach students to enter a phonetic key as well as a definition. For instance,

enough (e̱ <u>nuf</u>)—plenty, all that is needed

When a student reaches this point, he needs to become proficient at using the glossary of his book, and he needs to be introduced to a beginner's dictionary.

What skills must a child know to use a dictionary?

Step 1.   Can he say his ABC's accurately?

Step 2.   When shown a series such as g ___i, can he quickly supply the missing letter?

Step 3.   Can he alphabetize words by the first letter?

Step 4.   The second letter?

Step 5.   The third letter?

These skills are prerequisite to dictionary skills and need to be thoroughly mastered before the dictionary is taught. They can be taught together with second grade reading materials. When the student goes on to the dictionary, he needs to be given experiences where he will guess where a word will be. For example, Will he open the dictionary in the middle, front, or toward the end?

Teaching this skill can be almost fun. You say, "I'm going to say a word. You will tell me, Is it toward the beginning, middle, or end of the dictionary."

"The word is *back*. If you think it is at the beginning of the dictionary

signal . If you think it is in the middle, signal . If you think it is near the

end of the dictionary, signal ."

When students get good at this, have them practice opening dictionaries. They hold the dictionary up. You say a word. They decide if it's in the front, middle, or back before opening it.

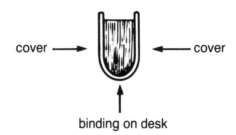

cover ⟶   ⟵ cover

binding on desk

Upon a signal, they try to open the dictionary at random to the place where the correct beginning letter will fall. It is fun to see whether they can hit the beginning letter on the first try. These types of experiences should be given many times until students form a habit of thinking before opening the dictionary.

Next the concept of guide words must be taught. The student needs to understand that the first guide word represents the first word on the page, while the other guide word represents the last word on the page.

Students need a lot of practice looking up words by using guide words. This is best done as a speed and power drill. The object of the drill is to see how fast you can locate a word. As the student gets better at it, it will be almost a game. He can plot his speed against that of other students, or he can plot against his own previous speed.

Dictionary skills can be poorly taught—as in the case where the student is given lists of words to look up and is asked to write down what he has found. The problem with this type of lesson is that it is deadly dull and guaranteed to turn off student interest and that the student may learn absolutely nothing. He may find the word by accident or someone will find it for him, or he can copy the information without reading it, or even if he reads it, one exposure is insufficient to teach a new word.

If your objective is to teach the student to use a dictionary, speed and power drills are most effective. You can do them easily with 4 to 8 students. If your objective is to teach word meaning, you will like the techniques described earlier in this chapter ("Teaching New Vocabulary") or the synonym game described next.

Thesaurus

The thesaurus is not always available in schools, but it should be. Paperback copies can be obtained very reasonably. One enjoyable student activity that encourages the learning of synonyms is a synonym game.

The Synonym Game

1. Make a game board—use a piece of bristol board (cardboard) approximately 18″ × 24″. Draw

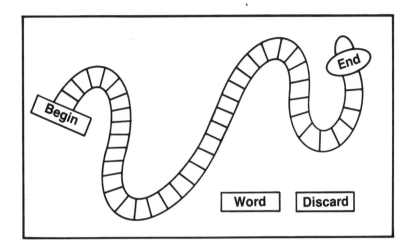

2. Make word cards. Choose words:
   a. that are appropriate to the age of the student (reading level of student) from his texts or from the *EDL Core Vocabulary* and
   b. that have one or more synonyms. Put one word on each card.

3. Make a master list that contains all the words (listed alphabetically) and all acceptable synonyms for each word.

4. Players (two is the best number, but three or four can play) put their markers or game pieces on begin square. The first player draws a card. He can move one space for each correct synonym he can name. (The other players check his responses for accuracy by looking at the master list.) If the player can name *all* of the synonyms given for the word, he can draw another card. If not, it is the next player's turn. The person who reaches the pot of gold at the end first is the winner.

A sample word list for a grade 3 to 4 student might be:

a ban don—leave, quit, surrender

ab surd—silly, foolish, stupid

ad e quate—enough, ample, plenty, sufficient

ad monish—warn, caution, scold

a dult—grown, mature

aid—assist, help, support

a maze—astonish, stun, surprise

a musing—entertaining, funny

an ger—rage, wrath, fury

an noy—disturb, bother, vex, irritate, irk

an swer—response, reply

bare—naked, nude

be wilder—perplex, mystify, puzzle, confuse, baffle
bluff—cliff, precipice

calm—peaceful, quiet, restful, soothing
cast—fling, toss, throw, hurl
choose—select, pick
chub by—fat, plump
clutch—grab, grasp, hold
clump—cluster, bunch, group
col lect—gather, accumulate, amass
com mence—begin, start
com mon—ordinary, usual
com plete—finish, accomplish, attain
com pose—create, make
cor rect—accurate, right, true

de cay—rot, spoil
dense—solid, thick
de part—exit, leave
des pise—hate, abhor, loathe
de vour—eat, consume
dot—spot, fleck, speck
dread ful—awful, terrible

e lim i nate—omit, erase, discard, shed, delete
emp ty—vacant, void, bare, hollow
en tire—whole, all
ex change—trade, swap

fab u lous—wonderful, terrific, super
fa tigue—weary, tired
frail—weak, delicate, breakable, fragile
fright—fearful, scared, terror, panic, alarm
glad—happy, joyful, delighted
glis ten—shine, glow, twinkle
gloom y—cheerless, dark, dismal, sad

If you decide to use the synonym game, it can become an IEP goal, for example:

> By June 1989, Jane will be able to give at least one synonym for 30 grade 3–4 words, not known on Jan. pretest.

The first few times that you play the game, it is not fun because the students don't know the words, but by the third or fourth time, they begin to enjoy it. If some of the words are known before introducing the game, that helps.

Indexes

Being able to use an index is a very useful skill. As the students' skills approach fifth grade level, it is wise to teach the skill.

Sample Lesson

Preplanning: Using the students' science or social studies text, make a list of eight questions, skipping around in the book. Be sure to check to see whether the key words in your questions appear in the index. The following is a portion of an index and a sample question to illustrate how to do this:

Portion of index	
Magnets and Magnetism	65–82
attraction/repulsion	69–72
electricity, making	74–78
magnetic field	68
lodestone	73
poles	66–67

Sample question: Explain how electromagnets work.

(The key word is *electromagnet.*) Students need to read questions until they are proficient at locating the key noun. Then they scan the index for that key word, locate the pages that apply, and turn to those pages to confirm that the information they are seeking is really there.

Once students become good at locating the key noun and finding the page numbers in an index, they can usually see the value of this skill in helping them answer questions, and then short, open-book tests become good ways to help students to prepare for a mastery test.

Card Catalog

Another valuable research skill is being able to use the card catalog to locate reference materials. When teaching this skill, we want to give the student experiences where he must actually use that information to get the book from the shelves.

To teach this skill, it takes some preplanning and lots of one-to-one practice. First, make a list of subjects, authors, and titles available in your library. On the day of the lesson, prior to class, check to see that the book is on the shelf. Later, in class, help the individual student to look up the card in the catalog and to go to the shelf to get the book. Each student will need many experiences of this sort to become proficient at the skill. By teaching one student thoroughly, then letting him teach two more students who subsequently teach others, you can help your class learn this skill. Students will also begin to pick up the Dewey Decimal System as they have the shelf experiences.

Maps and Atlases

One of our most serious deficits in American education today is found in our poor student knowledge of geography. Geography—maps, and so on—is a dull subject when taken in isolation.

Local travel companies often have travelogue films or tour books available that can help you enliven a geography lesson.

Allow students to plan imaginary trips to various places. Ask them to show the route they will take. They can use pictures from travel books to show what they saw while there. If you are able to find a travel agent near your school, a walking field trip to the agent's office may spark interest in learning about the world. A travel agent can make a good guest speaker.

Encyclopedias

As I teach, I sometimes get flashbacks to my own childhood. I can remember listening in rapture as my sixth grade teacher spoke to us about Egypt, pyramids, and pharaohs, showing us pictures and reading to us from an encyclopedia. Her eyes glowed as she added to the text from her recent trip there. I don't remember whether she said it or whether I extrapolated it, but it was clear to me that books such as encyclopedias could transport me to places where I might never be able to physically go—but I could know about them as though I had.

In choosing encyclopedias, we need ones with excellent and abundant illustrations, pictures, and so on. We also need to help students realize how much these books can do to enrich our lives. To send students to write [copy] a report using an encyclopedia article is to shortchange them. We need to help them use the encyclopedia in conjunction with other vibrant messages—films, filmstrips, and teacher enthusiasm.

6

WORKING WITH OLDER LEARNING-DISABLED STUDENTS

TEACHING STRATEGIES FOR SUCCESS

Learning-disabled students need to do the following:

1. Understand their particular learning problem
2. Be helped to develop strategies that will overcome that difficulty
3. Learn to be their own advocate

This approach should be taken as early as they are able to assimilate the information. Readiness for this kind of information varies from student to student—a mature eight-year-old who is motivated to do well in school can be helped. Certainly by seventh grade (and every year thereafter), each LD student should receive some instruction and practice in these strategies.

The sequence might include the following:

Step 1. "You have a learning disability. What do you think that means?" Generally they believe that they are dumb, or they have no idea what it means. Explain to them in very simple terms about their learning disability, as follows:

1. "You read and do math okay, but writing gives you a problem."
2. "You read and do math pretty well, but your memory is not too good; you lose things; you forget things."
3. "You're good at fixing things and drawing, but not as good with reading and math."

Choose one or more of these famous people to talk about. The one who most nearly has the student's problem is a good choice: Cher, the movie star, is dyslexic and can't read well. Tom Cruise, the movie star, is also dyslexic. Henry Winkler, "The Fonz," has problems with math. At the age of 10, Thomas Edison's teacher told his mother that it was a waste of time trying to teach him because he was so dumb. People in those days used candlepower to light their homes. Thomas Edison made the first electric light bulb. Albert Einstein was a strange child who did not do very well in school. Later he figured out the math that allows us to send spaceships into orbit.

Step 2. For older elementary students you may want to explain a bit about brain function. Point out to them that the kinds of things we expect of them in school are generally left-hemisphere functions. Right-brained children are often very valuable and creative people. If we can recognize these students in school and give them credit, their self-esteem will be preserved.

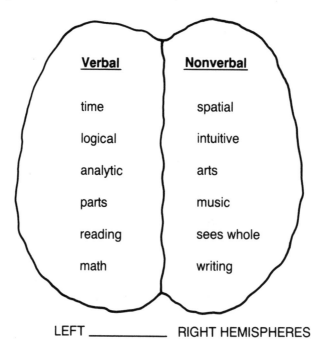

Verbal

time

logical

analytic

parts

reading

math

Nonverbal

spatial

intuitive

arts

music

sees whole

writing

LEFT _____ RIGHT HEMISPHERES

If we include right-brained activities in our lessons, learning is enhanced. One example of this is the use of rhythm and pitch to teach spelling.

Also point out that it's possible to be very good at one thing and very bad at another. Let them know that even in areas in which they do poorly, other parts of the brain can sometimes be trained to take over—but it takes persistence and courage.

Step 3. In this phase you want children to deal with their feelings—they may show denial, guilt, anger, depression (just as their parents did), and they need to be told, "It's okay to be angry," "It's not your fault." They should be encouraged to tell their war stories in a group so that they realize that others are feeling just as dumb and embarrassed. You may need to lead off with a war story of your own. "The stupidest thing I ever did was . . ." Tell it in detail and describe how you blew it. But then you should move on to how you overcame these feelings.

Give an example: there were two men who each lost a leg in the war. One man became a wimp and said, "Poor me." He took to his bed and wheelchair and never worked again. The second man also lost a leg, but he immediately started to use a prosthesis. Whenever he fell, he got up and tried again. In three years, he was walking without a cane, working at a job, and getting married. Ask: "What's the difference between these two men?"

Now you can move the student into searching for ways that courage and persistence can help them.

Step 4. Help students write a list of their strengths and weaknesses. Be sure that the number of their strengths exceed weaknesses.

Step 5. Teach students to acknowledge their weaknesses to others. One dyslexic student I taught got her skills up to near grade level, so she was dropped from the Rsp program. The next year at junior high, the science teacher was returning some test papers to his students, chastising them for their poor performance. As he stood above her and glared down at her, he said, "And what's your excuse, young lady?" In her most polite manner, she said sweetly, "I'm dyslexic." He was stunned. Later he confessed that he had not looked at her records, didn't know her history, and he apologized profusely. She was able to convince him that she could do the test if he'd just ask her the questions out loud. She got a B in the class.

Have the students practice admitting their disability until it sounds natural. "I have an auditory processing problem, and it makes it difficult for me to understand what you say to me, unless you talk slowly."

Step 6. Teach students to be their own advocate. The student herself needs to be trained to be her own advocate. The parent or resource specialist can ask the teacher to adjust the curriculum for a student. The teacher may resist this suggestion, but that same teacher may give in to the child who can request courteously,

"I'm learning-disabled, I need . . . Could you let me . . .?"

"I need to use a tape-recorder so I can replay your lecture."

"I need to know exactly what to study. Can you show me?"

"Could you help me make sure my notes contain all the information that I need to study?"

"I want to be successful—will you help me?"

Students can learn to say these things by practicing them.

Step 7. Teach students strategies for learning. To illustrate this concept, try looking at the following list for 20 seconds, and then try to reproduce it from memory:

jeep

pontiac

horse

oldsmobile

chevrolet

iris

ant

bean

ford

sloth

rose

How did you do it? Visualization of the entries? Classification by vehicle, animal, flower? A first-letter mnemonic like Jerry *put his old car in a barn for several reasons?* Or did you combine these methods in some way?

The point here is that students can be taught a variety of approaches to facilitate memory. We want each person to find the ones that work best for her (see Chapter 4 on memory and Chapter 5 on spelling).

Recently it was my privilege to attend a very fine seminar by Anita Archer. She described a program she and her colleague, Mary Gleason, have developed entitled *Skills for School Success*, which is available from Curriculum Associates, 5 Esquire Road, North Billerica, MA 01862–2589.

This program is a step-by-step fully scripted guide that teaches students (in grade 4 and up) organizational skills, behavioral skills, and academic skills that will markedly increase their chances for school success.

Step 8. Teaching students to take notes. Ideally notetaking can begin as soon as students read at grade 3 level or have enough phonics to support notetaking (know all sound combinations shown on the form "Student's Reminder for Decoding," in Chapter 6).

Sample Lesson in Notetaking Shorthand

Prerequisite skills: Visualization and verbalization, phonics training, memory training.

Anticipatory step: Write on board

2   da   we   r   2   lrn   to   rt   fstr

Say: "As soon as you know what this says, raise your hand." (When the majority of hands are up, ask students to give the answer in unison.)

Objective: Explain that good students take notes and that you are going to help them learn this skill so that they can make better grades.

Input: Using an overhead projector or a chalkboard, write:

The flow of water can be used to make electricity = 40 symbols

floing H_2O can   mak   ⚡   =   16   symbols

(symbol for water)   (symbol for electricity)

Let them know that they can devise their own shorthand system. The only requirement is that they be able to read it back. Explain that many people drop vowels and substitute symbols for common nouns. Small words, like *the*, *of*, are usually eliminated. Ask them to try to figure out these two messages:

t   gd   drnk   4
sumr   da

she   lvs   in   bg   hs
ner   bs   stp.

Pair them for guided practice. Put this message on the chalkboard and ask them to rewrite it in shorthand.

> "The teacher said that we would go on a field trip to Newport Beach in Sep-
> tember. We will ride a bus down and take the train back." (100 symbols)

Circulate and give help as needed. A kind of class agreement can be made on symbols. For example: The children can agree to use the following symbols:

W to mean we, h = he, sh = she, tha = they.

You may want to go back after they have worked for a few minutes and strike out all the unnecessary words: for example, /~~The~~ teacher said ~~that~~ we would go ~~on a~~ field trip to Newport Beach.

Put up the final product on a chart—original and shorthand.

> tech   sd   W   wd   go fld   trp   2   Nwpt   Bch   Spt.   1
> rd   bs   dn,   tak   tran   bk. (45 symbols)

On subsequent days, give them additional practice using paragraphs taken from texts and have them work in pairs.

Later when they get gd w/ shthnd, u cn strt hvg thm tak lkchr nots.

You can continue to stimulate them to do shorthand by giving them homework assignments to do (let them translate the text to shorthand).

Step 9. Demonstrate that they can read their notes. Students need to learn to read and ask themselves the following questions: Who? Where? What? When? How? Why?

They should be taught that usually the main idea will either be *first* or *last* in a paragraph. The technique that can be taught to a group or to an individual goes like this: First, read the paragraph once all the way through. Next, read the first sentence and last sentence. Then, read the paragraph through once more. Was the paragraph more about the first sentence or the last sentence? On paper, record the main idea. Also record who, where, what, when, how, and why.

Step 10. Teach students to obtain greater meaning from content texts. Students will get more out of a chapter of science and social studies if they are taught to routinely study it, as follows:

Preview. In phase one, they go through and read headings.

Focus. In this phase, they learn to ask the teacher for a list of the most crucial subjects.

Read. The students read a section and dissect that section making notes on who, where, what, when, how, and why. If there are study questions they answer them, and if they are not sure of their answer, they ask for clarification. Many students have difficulty asking for clarification. They fear that their peers will think that they are dumb or are showing off to please the teacher. I believe that if we began in grade 4 to teach these study strategies, we could eliminate this fear and turn our students into lifelong learners.

Review. At the end of a chapter, students should test one another prior to the formal test. This skill must be practiced.

Step 11. Teach students to be smarter test-takers. On multiple-choice tests, students should be able to move along without undue loss of time. First, they should answer all questions they are sure of and reserve questions needing further scrutiny with a ? in the margin. For puzzling questions, they should try to eliminate as many choices as they can. For example, if there are four answers to a question and you can eliminate one as being incorrect, your chance of getting the question right is 33 percent. If you can eliminate two answers, your chance of being right rises to 50 percent. Students should be told that very few things in our world happen all the time. Likewise, the word *never* generally eliminates an answer. Students should also be told to watch the clock. Five minutes before the test ends, they should check to be sure that they have marked an answer to every question even if they are guessing. They may pick up some extra points by guessing.

Step 12. Teach students to enhance their own image. Students need to be shown how to improve their skills with people. In school and on the job, teachers should stress the rewards for the following:

1. Dependability

2. Punctuality

3. Preparedness (being equipped with materials to do the job)

4. Appropriate dress

5. Pleasing manner

6. Willingness to do what is asked.

In one experiment, students who were failing were taken for "special tutoring." Teachers believed that this was to be for academic tutoring. Actually, what was done was that the students were given pointers and practice in the above areas. In addition, they were able to role-play situations that their instructors set up, and eventually they learned to "read" what the teacher wanted and valued. In the next marking period, every student's grade improved. Though nothing was taught to improve their academics, they learned a lot about improving how they were perceived. They learned that this was of benefit to them in school and would also benefit them later—on the job.

A large part of evaluation is subjective. Students need to know that. It is also important to teach students to say, "I've never done that before, but I'm sure I can learn it if you will show me how." They should be cautioned not to pretend to know, especially where high-tech machinery is involved. If they believe that they can use the equipment, they should learn to say, "I think I can do it, but will you watch me and give me pointers?"

There is value to having a panel of employers talk to classes regarding what characteristics make a good employee and allowing the students to ask questions.

UNDERSTANDING THE CHANGING NEEDS
OF THE INTERMEDIATE LD STUDENT

The average thirteen- to fifteen-year-old spends little time thinking of school. On becoming a teenager, his vistas expand rapidly—he's bigger; he's realizing that he can do more; he's aware that there is far more "out there" than he thought. His hormonal system is coming into play. His interest in the opposite sex and in his own sexuality is a distracting influence. The teenager is a sensation-oriented creature. Often his desire for new sensations puts him on a collision course with danger. Lacking mature judgment, he may experiment with drugs (including alcohol), sex, and fast vehicles, thus trying to assert his growing independence without considering the consequences. Luckily, we do not get negative consequences 100 percent of the time.

The predicament of the early teen is that suddenly his body is more like that of an adult than a child. Changes are happening from the inside, but more important, changes are coming from the outside. Because of his new body, people expect him to practice self-control. As a teenager, you're expected to be graceful, which is not easy. You're expected to be articulate and eloquent, yet you've got the vocabulary of a sixth grader. You're expected to display yourself, know who you are, and what you want. You feel under stress because you think that you have to look good. School contests for who has the nicest eyes, the nicest legs are a big mistake because it makes all but a select few feel ugly. Such contests are also totally irrelevant to learning. Indeed, concentrating on cosmetic beauty is counterproductive to education. Likewise, school dances requiring fancy dress and a partner are distractions from the educational process. This kind of socialization will eventually happen without the school's promoting it. Contests stressing academic skills would be appropriate since the school's primary function is education.

Going to school is something that the teenager has been doing for several years. It's a dull and tedious business, but most children have found ways to cope. They have learned the limits to how much they can goof off without flunking or getting a referral, and they know how to appease their parents.

In junior high school, there is a caste system—the geeks, the socies, and the stoners, as follows:

1. Socies are joiners. They are looking to fit in. They try to get in sports and clubs. They want to be cute and popular.

2. Stoners are in the system but are not a part of it. They band together for survival, to be seen as being "bad." Stoners are rebellious.

3. Geeks include people who do not fit in with socies or stoners either by their choice or because they have been rejected.

Within the LD population, we find a few geeks and socies, but primarily we find stoners. Stoners are children who invest little in learning. They do not relate to traditional teachers. For them, the teaching role must shift from "oracle" to "mentor." The mentor is a facilitator, a helper, or a guide, but not necessarily a friend.

ADJUSTING AND DEVELOPING CURRICULUM TO MEET STUDENT INTEREST

The recurring theme I hear from junior high school students is, "Why do I need to do or learn this?" The material taught must either be obviously useful or more exciting than their social lives to get the junior high student's attention.

The novel and the relevant undertakings are more likely to gain a student's attention. Projects in the community fit into this category. One such project undertaken by students was the painting and repairing of an elderly woman's home. Another was a day where students sat in for various city officials (the mayor, police chief, and so on). A third project was meeting with and talking with former POW's about their war experiences.

Historical plays and role-playing can be dynamic stuff. The teacher writes the play. The students act it in front of an audience. If the local TV station is taping the show, the students come alive and become really involved.

Lessons that tune into individual student temperament are very effective. Allow students doing research to join an interest group of their choice—for example, great battles of the Civil War, the architecture and customs of the Civil War South, the plight of the slave in contrast to the needs of the slave-holder. At the end of a period of research (they may work in pairs or alone, as they choose), each student reports on an interesting aspect of the whole. A synopsis (a whole group report) can be generated and printed, with a copy placed in the school library listing the names of the contributors.

Several programs are designed to stimulate critical thinking. Teaching students to solve problems and evaluate solutions can produce a lot of learning. An example of such a question is, "Examine Sherman's march to the sea. Was this a good idea or not? Be prepared to justify your answer. Is there a situation where this tactic might be employed today?"

In a civics class, more recent events can be topics for similar sorts of evaluation. Allowing students to design their own exams can be a novel experience.

One of the primary needs of intermediate secondary students is to be with their peers—to bounce ideas off their peers. Cooperative learning offers an excellent opportunity for students to do just that.

Unfortunately, many school districts make a concerted effort to have LD students follow the core curriculum followed by all junior high students. The shortcoming of this approach is that many LD students still need much reading instruction, and the complaint of their teachers is that the day is too short to provide what they need. Time needed to teach the critical survival skill of reading is being diverted into teaching less critical skills.

DEVELOPING VOCATIONAL AWARENESS, PREVOCATIONAL SKILLS, AND VOCATIONAL SKILLS

Intermediate school or junior high school is a good place to develop vocational awareness, and many districts, including mine, do require programs covering the following:

1. Types of occupations
2. Types of desirable work behavior
3. Filling out sample employment forms and role-playing interviews

Most of my colleagues, however, feel that they are totally without preparation to teach in this area. The lack of availability of good texts in this area is also a criticism frequently heard.

THE ART OF COUNSELING INTERMEDIATE STUDENTS

In talking with colleagues and junior high students, we find that teenagers relate best to their peers and invariably turn to their peers for advice. Rarely do they seek or want help from adults. When and if they do, however, there are some guidelines to follow. Be aware that lawsuits can be filed for both your sins of commission and omission, so you will want to protect yourself as best you can.

When you find yourself in a room alone with a student, it is wise to keep the door open. If it appears that the student is going to confide very intimate information, often signaled by the remark, "If I tell you something, promise not to tell," it is wise to say to the student, "No, I'm sorry, I cannot make that promise. There are some kinds of information I *must* tell."[4] Tell the student that you are willing to listen to her concern and that you will do all you can to help her with her problem, but if she is going to share her problem with you, she has to have enough trust in you to accept your handling of the problem.

When a problem is confided, it is best to let the student talk at length about it. Don't interrupt; *do* write down clarification questions so that you can ask them later. These notes will make you a more active listener.

Sometimes a student does not need or want help with her problem. She just wants to tell someone. The pressure she is feeling may be alleviated by this catharsis. So when a student has finally finished unloading, you may want to say, "Why did you want to tell me about this?" and if appropriate, "What do you hope I can do to help you?"

Sometimes it is appropriate to help a student look at her fears and get them out in the open. "If _____ happened, what would be the worst scenario that you could foresee? Could you handle that? How?" You do need, however, to ask the other side: "If _____ happened, what would be the best scenario you could see? Are there ways we can act to move toward achieving the best scenario? How can I help?"

Occasionally, as a counselor, you may see something in a situation that the student did not mention. You can say one of the following:

---

[4]In many states, teachers must report child abuse—whether suspected or verifiable—or risk a fine and a jail sentence for failure to report. Likewise, situations that are life threatening—suicide or abortion—need to be shared with your superior and ultimately with the student's parents.

"I wonder if _____?"

"Have you ever considered _____?"

"Is it possible that _____?"

"I had a similar experience once and I _____."

"If I understand correctly, you feel _____."

As an adult, you may use your repertory of experiences to be helpful. You can say, "Perhaps _____ feels this way." As an adult, you may be able to help the student understand parental feelings: "You feel _____, but your parents may feel _____."

The student may or may not choose to follow your advice, should you give any. If it doesn't feel right to her, she won't. You need to respect this decision—unless it involves a life-threatening problem like suicide or abortion.

If a learning-disabled student wants to attend college, it would seem appropriate for a teacher or counselor to put her in touch with the college of her choice, beginning to plan in the eleventh grade toward her acceptance. (See the list of sources of help at end of this handbook.) A covering letter from the school to the college, sharing of information (release required), could be of great assistance to the student. Likewise, a referral to the state department of vocational rehabilitation may be helpful.

THE ART OF COUNSELING SECONDARY STUDENTS

Like younger teenagers, high school students usually seek help from their friends. Peer-tutoring programs sponsored and designed by the individual high schools can be very beneficial. In the local school, it works this way. Students interested in being peer counselors take an elective class—80 or more hours of lectures covering a variety of topics. They have an opportunity to demonstrate their skills. Students wishing a peer counselor are given one. Confidentiality exists on all subjects except potential suicide. The peer counselor's job is to listen and help the student explore her alternatives. If peer counselors feel at a loss to deal with a problem, they can seek guidance from a trained adult.

HELPING PARENTS COPE

Counseling parents is another role we must often assume. You need to do the following:

1. Listen actively—making notes.

2. Ascertain what kind of information they need from you.

3. Provide information. Of particular importance is being able to explain to parents what expectations are "normal" for the age of their child.

If you feel that the counseling needed by the family exceeds what you have the ability or time to give, simply say, "I'm sorry, I feel that I can't help you, but I would like to suggest that you call _____ for assistance." Suggest a private or public counseling agency.

UNDERSTANDING THE NEEDS OF THE SECONDARY STUDENT

In ninth grade, the teenager regains some social equilibrium—she has either been able to fit in (socies/stoners) or she hasn't (geeks), but she now faces a new disquieting element. She realizes that she has only three years left in which to decide what she wants to do after graduation.

Like the junior high student, the secondary student wants lessons that are novel or relevant to life, but she will also try hard to meet school system demands that she must demonstrate certain competencies in order to graduate.

Many secondary students are looking for their first jobs. They are open to help in how to go about finding a job. Some school districts have highly developed vocational programs. My district, for example, employs two full-time vocational counselors who locate jobs and try to match students to the jobs they seek. There is an incentive for employers. The district pays the students' wages for several weeks. At the end of this time, the employers can either opt to retain the employees and pay their wages or release them.

In California, we have regional occupational centers that offer, without cost, training in a variety of fields: auto diagnostics, animal care, cosmetology, barbering, banking, business office technology, construction, electronics, floristry, grocery retail, medical assisting, nursery or horticulture, nursery and child care, printing, recreational and instructional aide training, restaurant occupations, and warehousing. This training is open to anyone 16 years or older, including adults.

COLLEGE AND VOCATIONAL TRAINING

Many colleges have offices and counselors who help LD students plan their course of study since LD students may have to be judged by different standards. For students who do not go on to college, in addition to the regional occupational programs and the vocational rehabilitation service, there are sheltered workshops. The armed services also offer opportunities for vocational training and further schooling.

7

A CALL TO ACTION

The following are some appalling statistics to be reckoned with:

60 million Americans read below eighth grade level.

85 percent of juveniles coming before the courts are functionally illiterate.

50 percent of prisoners are illiterate.

The cost to society of this illiteracy exceeds $200 billion a year.[5] Parents blame educators. Educators blame parents. What's wrong here?

It is no one's fault. But since the field of education for the learning disabled is in its infancy, we need to increase society's awareness of the condition. Many people do not know what a learning disability is. They sometimes confuse it with mental retardation. Television could be the agent for dispelling this ignorance. We need scripts in story form that show what it is like to have a learning disability. We need documentaries to provide helpful information. Short commercials by well-known celebrities who are learning-disabled could help.

It is sad to say, but nevertheless true, that our teacher training and physician training institutions also need to increase their offerings in the field of learning disabilities. By means of continuing education courses, older teachers and physicians could become more informed about learning disabilities.

I would like to see a change in federal regulations that would allow us to identify and serve learning-disabled students when they need help rather than waiting for a severe discrepancy (between their achievement and potential) to occur. By serving them earlier, perhaps we could prevent a feeling of failure and loss of self-esteem. I would also like to see the following changes in our educational system:

1. Governmental support of good quality day-care centers. Many young children need good preschool experiences, especially those children from areas of cultural deprivation.

2. Prekindergarten screening of all students. Those students not ready for academics would receive appropriate developmental experiences.

3. A better teacher to pupil ratio. In kindergarten through third grade, a ratio of one to twelve would be ideal.

4. Parent education programs are needed at a variety of levels:

---

[5]These statements were made by Jonathan Kozol, author of *Illiterate America*, on the *Phil Donahue Show*, June 1988.

    a. During pregnancy, both parents could learn what to expect and do during the critical years from birth to age 3.

    b. As children enter schools, parents could be told ways in which they could help their child. They need to realize that the average child proceeds through school in 13 years (including kindergarten) but that some children—at least one in five—need 14 or 15 years to make the same journey. They need to be told that retention is not a failure but is rather an opportunity for students to grow in their skills.

    c. Ongoing programs should be established to give guidance so that parents can cope more adequately with their children's changing needs.

    d. In high school, we need to have classes in parenting so that students have a realistic view of their responsibilities and can decide whether they wish to make the commitment that parenting involves.

5. An alternative route to teaching for the primary grades. I am convinced that some people are born teachers because I have had some highly competent assistants who were only high school graduates. A five-year, on-the-job apprentice teacher program could prepare them to teach the primary grades while lowering the teacher to pupil ratio. It could be done without great cost.

6. Extension of the school year. All schools would offer year-round schooling—nine weeks on, four off. During the four-week periods, two kinds of intersessions could be offered: an enrichment strand and a remedial strand. The enrichment strand would be optional. The remedial strand would be mandatory for lagging students (one-to-one help would be given).

7. We also need to do a better job of counseling these students so that they understand the specific nature of their problem and have strategies to succeed in life. We need to protect their self-esteem so that they realize that they have personal value and worth.

8. Beginning in ninth grade, the curriculum would offer classes in elementary plumbing; car maintenance and repair; restaurant and cafeteria skills; typing, filing, and bookkeeping; first aid and CPR; child development and care; agriculture; elementary home repair and carpentry; and understanding the laws. The school day would be expanded from the present six hours to eight hours, including a one-hour study hall with lots of tutorial help available.

    By the end of 10th grade, every student would have been given an interest inventory, an aptitude test, and counseling by trained counselors as to career fields and the training opportunities available.

    We would routinely provide job training at the secondary educational level. Occupationally, in our society there is room to accommodate all sorts of handicapped workers. We need to carefully analyze the job requirements for each position and guide the LD person into fields where they can safely and successfully perform.

For those students who want to go to college, preparation for the SAT exam would be given.

Where appropriate, the vocational rehabilitation service and sheltered workshops would be brought into play.

9. All high schools would train and encourage peer counseling. Prerequisite to being a counselor would be successful completion of eighty hours of classroom training involving role-playing. This training would be designed to familiarize students with reactions to stress and would cover subjects of drug abuse, child abuse, divorce, pregnancy, and suicide.

10. Financial incentives for students should be offered to students to remain in school.

Finally, I feel that we need a national repository for information relating to the education of the learning disabled that would publish a newsletter available without cost to all teachers. (On their limited salaries, many teachers feel unable to belong to voluntary professional organizations.)

Currently the National Information Center for Handicapped Children and Youth does try to meet that need with a newsletter. You can request to be put on their mailing list (see the list of sources of help at the end of this handbook).

In conclusion, I would like to quote from pages 5 and 6 of the report, *A Nation At Risk:*[6]

> Our nation is at risk. Our once unchallenged preeminence in commerce, industry, science and technological innovation is being overtaken by our competitors. Throughout the world . . . the educational foundations of our society are presently being eroded by a rising tide of mediocrity which threatens our very future as a Nation and a people. What was unimaginable a generation ago has begun to occur—others are matching and surpassing our educational attainments.
>
> If an unfriendly foreign power had attempted to impose on America the mediocre educational performance that exists today, we might well have viewed it as an act of war. As it stands, we have allowed this to happen to ourselves.
>
> Our society and its educational institutions seem to have lost sight of the basic purposes of schooling, and of the high expectations and disciplined effort needed to attain them.
>
> That we have compromised this commitment is, upon reflection, hardly surprising, given the multitude of often conflicting demands we have placed on our Nation's schools and colleges. They are routinely called on to provide solutions to personal, social and political problems that the home and other institutions either will not or cannot resolve. We must understand that these demands on our schools and colleges often exact an educational cost as well as a financial one.

---

[6]*A Nation at Risk: The Imperative for Educational Reform*, a report by the National Commission on Excellence in Education, April 1983.

This report, therefore, is as much an open letter to the American people as it is a report to the Secretary of Education. We are confident that the American people, properly informed, will do what is right for their children and for the generations to come.

Statistic: 51 percent of learning-disabled youngsters do not complete high school.

Children are our nation's most valuable resource. As teachers, we can, individually and collectively, make contributions to the well-being of this precious asset. We can help children to strive for excellence, thereby reaching their individual maximum potential. This, in turn, will restore vitality to our Nation.

Appendices

1: Glossary

2: Test Materials

3: Sources of Help (Organizations)

4: Educator's Checklist: Observable Clues to Classroom Vision Problems

Glossary

Agnosia. The inability to process information through one of the senses, even though the receiving organ does not seem to be impaired—for example, the child who must use lip-reading techniques to discriminate an *m* from an *n* because he cannot distinguish the difference, although an audiometric examination shows a normal hearing pattern.

Alexia. A total inability to read due to some cerebral damage. It may be an inability of a child to learn to read, or it may occur suddenly in adults, as in the case of a trauma or a stroke.

Anomia. The inability to recall names of objects or words.

Aphasia. The inability to acquire or understand oral language. This may range from a total nonuse of oral language to the person being able to understand what is said to her but she cannot use language herself. The condition occurs due to damage in the brain's speech areas.

Apraxia. A disturbance in motor movements that is reflected in poor gross or fine motor control.

Closure. The ability to fill in gaps—for example, to look at a part of a thing and recognize it as the whole (such as half a tree), or to fill in a blank in a sentence with the correct word.

Constancy. The inability to recognize the sameness of shapes and sounds if they appear in another context from the one in which they were learned.

Dyscalculia. The inability to perform math operations. A sample symptom is transposing the order of numbers—36 is 63.

Dysgraphia. The inability to control fine movements of the hand so that written work is of extremely poor quality.

Dyslexia (similar to alexia, but different in degree). Dyslexia is an extremely slow acquisition of reading skills, but alexia is a total inability to read.

Electroencephalogram (EEG). A nonpainful medical procedure whereby neurological brain damage may be discovered.

Epilepsy. A neurological disorder now called *seizure disorder*. Seizures may range from being very mild (virtually unnoticeable) to severe (resulting in loss of consciousness and violent spasms). Most seizures can be controlled by medication.

Figure-ground distraction. The subject is unable to focus his attention on a task due to distracting influences (visual or auditory) in the environment. For example, many children require a marker when reading to blot out the distraction created by other words on the page.

Impulsivity. Acting on impulse, with no prior consideration of the possible untoward consequences.

Laterality. The inability to distinguish left from right sides of the body. This confusion can be overcome with skillful teaching directed at developing an awareness.

Modalities. The channels through which we perceive—visual, auditory, or tactile (touch).

Perception. Taking in information through our senses and processing that information in such a way that it has meaning to us.

Perseveration. The continuation of an activity beyond the saturation point; an inability to stop an activity.

Phonetics. The study of the sounds of letters and groups of letters.

Prader-Willi syndrome. A rare genetic disorder occasionally seen in LD children. Presenting symptoms are obesity and overeating.

Spatial disorder. An inability to conceptualize oneself as the body relates to other objects, time, or place.

Tourette's syndrome. A rare disorder occasionally seen in LD children. Presenting symptoms are tics, mouth noises (profanity or animal noises), and hyperactivity.

Test Materials

Brigance Inventory (American Guidance Services, Inc., Publishers Building, Circle Pines, MN 55014)

California Adaptive Behavior Scale, 1984 (Planet Press Enterprises, P.O. Box 3477, Newport Beach, CA 92663)

Draw-A-Person (Harcourt Brace Jovanovich, Inc., 757 Third Avenue, New York, NY 10017)

Key Math Test (American Guidance Services, Inc., Publishers Building, Circle Pines, MN 55014)

Peabody Individual Achievement Test (American Guidance Services, Inc., Publishers Building, Circle Pines, MN 55014)

Wechsler Intelligence Scale for Children (The Psychological Corporation, 757 Third Avenue, New York, NY 10017)

Wide-Range Achievement Test (Guidance Associates of Delaware, Inc., 1526 Gelpin Avenue, Wilmington, DE 19806)

Woodcock Reading Test (American Guidance Services, Inc., Publishers Building, Circle Pines, MN 55014)

Sources of Help

Allergy Foundation of America, 118–35 Queens Blvd., Forest Hills, NY 11375.

American Coalition of Citizens with Disabilities, 494 Westchester Avenue, Yonkers, NY 10707.

Association for Children with Learning Disabilities (ACLD), 4156 Library Road, Pittsburgh, PA 15234 (list of colleges and universities that accept students with learning disabilities).

Closer Look/Parents Campaign for Handicapped Children, 1201 16th Street, N.W., Suite 233, Washington, DC 20036.

Council for Exceptional Children, 1920 Association Drive, Reston, VA 22091 (journal and other information on LD).

Council for Learning Disabilities, P.O. Box 40303, Overland Park, KS 66204 (journal).

Crane-Reynolds, Inc., 9327 A Katy Freeway, Suite 327, Houston, TX 77024 (seminars on behavioral management; social skills curriculum for grades 1–12).

Directory of Educational Facilities and Services for the Learning Disabled, 12th ed. (Academic Therapy Publications, 1987).

Educational Testing Service, ATP Services for Handicapped Students, CN 6400, Princeton, NJ 08541–6400.

Epilepsy Foundation of America, 4351 Garden City Grove, Landover, MD 20785 (pamphlet).

Foundation for Children with Learning Disabilities, P.O. Box 2929, Grand Central Station, New York, NY 10016.

Irlen Institute for Perceptual and Learning Disabilities, P.O. Box 7175, Long Beach, CA 90807.

Lovejoy's College Guide for the Learning Disabled (Simon & Schuster, 1985, 1230 Avenue of the Americas, New York, NY 10020).

National Information Center for Handicapped Children and Youth (NICHCY), P.O. Box 1492, Washington, DC 20013 (newsletter and pamphlets for parents).

National Network of Learning-Disabled Adults, 808 North 82 Street, Suite F2, Scottsdale, AZ 85257.

Orton Dyslexia Society, 724 York Road, Baltimore, MD 21204.

President's Committee on Employment of the Handicapped, 1111 20th Street N.W., 6th floor, Washington, DC 20210 (free pamphlets).

Skyer Consultation Center, P.O. Box 121, Rockaway Park, NY 11694.

Task Force on Education for the Handicapped, Inc., 812 East Jefferson, South Bend, IN 46617.

Team of Advocates for Special Kids (TASK), 1800 East LaVeta, Orange, CA 92666.

Time-Out to Enjoy, Inc., 715 Lake Street, Suite 100, Oak Park, IL 60301.

Tourette's Syndrome Association, 41–02 Bill Blvd., Bayside, NY 11361.

Educator's Checklist of Clues to Vision Problems

EDUCATOR'S CHECKLIST

OBSERVABLE CLUES TO CLASSROOM VISION PROBLEMS

Student's
Name _____ Date _____

1. **APPEARANCE OF EYES:**
   One eye turns in or out at any time _____
   Reddened eyes or lids _____
   Eyes tear excessively _____
   Encrusted eyelids _____
   Frequent styes on lids _____

2. **COMPLAINTS WHEN USING EYES AT DESK:**
   Headaches in forehead or temples _____
   Burning or itching after reading or desk work _____
   Nausea or dizziness _____
   Print blurs after reading a short time _____

3. **BEHAVIORAL SIGNS OF VISUAL PROBLEMS:**
   A. *Eye Movement Abilities (Ocular Motility)*
      Head turns as reads across page _____
      Loses place often during reading _____
      Needs finger or marker to keep place _____
      Displays short attention span in reading or copying _____
      Too frequently omits words _____
      Repeatedly omits "small" words _____
      Writes up or down hill on paper _____
      Rereads or skips lines unknowingly _____
      Orients drawings poorly on page _____
   B. *Eye Teaming Abilities (Binocularity)*
      Complains of seeing double (diplopia) _____
      Repeats letters within words _____
      Omits letters, numbers or phrases _____
      Misaligns digits in number columns _____
      Squints, closes or covers one eye _____
      Tilts head extremely while working at desk _____
      Consistently shows gross postural deviations at all desk activities _____
   C. *Eye-Hand Coordination Abilities*
      Must feel of things to assist in any interpretation required _____
      Eyes not used to "steer" hand movements (extreme lack of orientation, placement of words or drawings on page) _____
      Writes crookedly, poorly spaced: cannot stay on ruled lines _____

Misaligns both horizontal and vertical series of numbers _____
Uses his hand or fingers to keep his place on the page _____
Uses other hand as "spacer" to control spacing and alignment on page _____
Repeatedly confuses left-right directions _____

   D. *Visual Form Perception (Visual Comparison, Visual Imagery, Visualization)*
      Mistakes words with same or similar beginnings _____
      Fails to recognize same word in next sentence _____
      Reverses letters and/or words in writing and copying _____
      Confuses likenesses and minor differences _____
      Confuses same word in same sentence _____
      Repeatedly confuses similar beginnings and endings of words _____
      Fails to visualize what is read either silently or orally _____
      Whispers to self for reinforcement while reading silently _____
      Returns to "drawing with fingers" to decide likes and differences _____
   E. *Refractive Status (Nearsightedness, Farsightedness, Focus Problems, etc.)*
      Comprehension reduces as reading continued; loses interest too quickly _____
      Mispronounces similar words as continues reading _____
      Blinks excessively at desk tasks and/or reading; not elsewhere _____
      Holds book too closely; face too close to desk surface _____
      Avoids all possible near-centered tasks _____
      Complains of discomfort in tasks that demand visual interpretation _____
      Closes or covers one eye when reading or doing desk work _____
      Makes errors in copying from chalkboard to paper on desk _____
      Makes errors in copying from reference book to notebook _____
      Squints to see chalkboard, or requests to move nearer _____
      Rubs eyes during or after short periods of visual activity _____
      Fatigues easily; blinks to make chalkboard clear up after desk task _____

OBSERVER'S SUGGESTIONS:

Signed (Print) _____
(Encircle): Teacher; Nurse; Remedial Teacher; Psychologist; Vision Consultant; Other.

Phone _____

Address _____

_____